Making Friends with Ghosts

A MOTHER'S UNUSUAL JOURNEY OF SELF-DISCOVERY

MALLORY CYWINSKI

BEYOND THE FRAY
Publishing

ISBN 13: 978-1-954528-59-8

Cover design: Disgruntled Dystopian Publications

Beyond The Fray Publishing, a division of Beyond The Fray, LLC, San Diego, CA

www.beyondthefraypublishing.com

BEYOND THE FRAY

Publishing

CONTENTS

Prologue   1

PART ONE

1. Paranormal Party of One, Please RSVP   7
2. Hello, Darkness   13
3. Little Recoveries, Again and Again   23
4. First Taste of the Paranormal   29
5. The Beginning: Fort Mifflin   33
6. Awkwardly Repeat After Me: "I'm a Paranormal
   Investigator"   39
7. The Cost of Paranormal Investigating   43
8. A Hot Take on Paranormal Equipment   47
9. Joining the ParaCommunity   51
10. Notes on Fear   53

PART TWO

11. Secret Spooky Roommate   61
12. First Things First   65
13. Selma Mansion   69
14. Elks Lodge   85
15. Pennhurst State School and Hospital   93
16. Samuel Miller Mansion   101
17. The Shanley Hotel   109
18. Inn at Herr Ridge and Devil's Den on the
    Battlefield   117
19. Aaron Burr House   131
20. Bube's Brewery and Restaurant   137
21. The Hinsdale House   147
22. Wildwood Sanitarium   159

PART THREE

23. "Sorry, occupied!"   165
24. Haunted Cafés Are my Favorite   169
25. McCoole's at the Red Lion Inn   171
26. The Seven Stars Inn   175
27. Brinton Lodge   177
28. The Hotel Bethlehem   181
29. The Sun Inn   187
30. Salem Pioneer Village   191
31. Eastern State Penitentiary   195
32. Philadelphia Zoo   199
33. Pottsgrove Manor   203
34. Fonthill Castle   207
35. Baldwin's Book Barn   211
36. Frick's Lock Ghost Town   215
37. Rhoads Opera House   219
38. Valley Forge National Park   225
39. The Congress Hotel   231
40. Fort William Henry (and a Haunted Vacation
    Home?)   235
41. East Martello Museum, Home to Robert
    the Doll   243
42. Death, Grief, and Cemetery Exploration   247
43. Key West Cemetery   255
44. The Perils & Positives of Social Media   261

PART FOUR

45. Lessons from Ghosts   273

Final Thoughts, For Now   285
Afterword   291
Photos   295
Acknowledgments   305
References (& Resources for Your Independent
Rabbit Hole Research)   307
About the Author   315

For Cade & Maya

and tired moms everywhere

PROLOGUE

It was about eleven in the evening or so as I stood in our "safe room" at the dingy hotel in rural New York, clutching a Styrofoam cup of watery coffee. Clumps of powdered creamer floated across the top as I idly stirred it, taking a moment to roll out the kinks in my neck. There's nothing particularly "safe" about a safe room on a paranormal investigation – mostly it's just the room with all the lights on, where everyone dumps their bags so we don't have to drag all our equipment and overnight gear with us as we travel from room to room. I suppose calling the room "safe," labeling it as such, gives us all the façade of a breathing space, where we can turn off for a moment and rally ourselves and our energy for the following sessions of attempting to talk to ghosts. At this point in the night, we had just broken from one such session without much action, so to speak.

We'd been at the notoriously haunted Shanley Hotel for about five hours now, and even if the coffee wasn't top-notch, it was hot, and it had caffeine in it. I love paranormal investigations, but as the mother of two young kids, staying up past midnight isn't my strong suit, no matter what spooky uniden-tified sounds we were hearing. I was casually chatting with my friend – a blonde, chipper psychic medium I had known for about seven months by that point – as we willed the coffee to flood our veins as fast as possible.

Everyone in the group of eight people we had brought with us to this small, paint-chipped hotel in the sleepy town of Napanoch, New York, was a trusted friend or a friend of a friend. She and I were sipping from our cups, chatting about take-out food, of all things, when she briefly leaned down toward the table to my left. As she bent, our chatter trailed off, and I zoned out, staring down the hallway leading out of the great room we were in. Along that short hallway was the door to the bathroom, with the mirror scrying room just past that, the now-closed door to the upstairs brothel area to the right. Beyond the brothel door was the entry to the dormitory-style overnight rooms, what was once a "gentlemen's club" in days gone by. At that moment, a billowing figure in white bustled by, from left to right.

The figure was very tall – extraordinarily tall, actually – with legs that moved one after the other under the fabric of its clothing – loose pants? A dress? My mind emptied as I immedi-ately called out, "Who is that? Who is that?" Somehow everyone else in the room behind me, either grabbing a snack or talking with other group members, had seen nothing. There had been a pair chatting at the dining table just steps from the hallway entrance, but their chairs had been facing us, backs to the hallway as they sat. My feet propelled me toward what I had seen before my brain had made the decision to do so. My mind was suddenly spinning through so many thoughts I was barely conscious of each as I approached the hallway thresh-old. Yes, I was mildly fatigued – but not anywhere near so tired as to hallucinate a full and detailed figure. I nearly dropped my coffee from trembling hands as I rushed down the short hallway to try to catch the fleeing figure that had, in my rational mind, obviously been a person trying to play a hoax on my group. I saw nothing. The entrance door to the brothel stairwell remained closed, but that was irrelevant – the figure had clearly moved past that door into the gentlemen's club, a large open room that had no exit but an emergency door at the far end, still shut and locked, without the curtain in front disturbed. I spun around and checked every corner, under and behind each of the beds in the room – nothing. By that time, as I slowly walked back out to the safe room in a daze, I knew in my gut, and from the raised hairs on every inch of my body, that I had come to the Shanley Hotel to see ghosts, and I had, in fact, seen one.

PART ONE

"LET YOUR FREAK FLAG FLY HIGH,
SO THE OTHER FREAKS CAN FIND
YOU."

CHAPTER 1

PARANORMAL PARTY OF ONE, PLEASE RSVP

I 'm a wife and mother, I own a rescue dog, I read way too many books, and I'm a paranormal investigator. I prefer coffee over tea, mountains over the beach, and if my freak flag literally existed, there would be a ghost smack-dab in the middle of it. My path to the paranormal covers a very long stretch of my life, but a few years ago I jumped in with both feet and decided to openly own my "weird" interests and start investigating haunted spaces myself instead of merely watching others do it on TV and the internet. Now, as I approach middle age, I feel more comfortable in my own skin than I ever have before, and so much of that feeling is from allowing myself to explore my unusual passions. I wish it hadn't taken me so long to do so, but I also think that timing is everything, and the "when" of how things unfold is as impor-tant as the "what." For me, embracing the strange, neglected outlier branches of my interests came at a time in my life when I needed it most. Perhaps I needed the extra drive born of desperation to make that final push to take action. In many intervals of my life, I've grappled with the Dark in lots of ways, but ironically, it was a different form of darkness that saved me from being the sad, stagnant person I didn't want to be. Nor the mother I wanted for my children.

Many paranormal investigators have a go-to answer when they are inevitably asked "How did you get interested in the paranormal?" and it usually begins with something along the lines of "When I was a child..." and ends in a recollection of some unexplainable phenomena they witnessed at a young age. Sometimes they claim to have seen the same ghostly apparition walk the hallways at their grandmother's house over and over, or their childhood imaginary friend was more than a figment of their young mind, or they just had gut feelings about certain places from their youth. Then, as they grew into adulthood, interest in the paranormal was just part of their lives, a given. Though it took me a long time to fully commit to my interest in ghosts, my paranormal journey did in fact begin when I was a child. Not only that, but it started with a classic horror trope: a creepy doll.

My dad used to go on business trips all over the world, and it became a tradition for him to bring me back a doll from wherever he had been. I delighted in my collection; I had tall spindly-legged dolls and small, stiff plastic dolls with painted lips. Once, when he returned, he presented me with a little Navajo-style doll, about seven inches in height. Her face lacked much expression, but her little blue velvet dress had lovely intricate beadwork, and her black hair was bound into a low bun at the back of her head. After a few days of her role as guest of honor at tea parties with other toys in attendance, I nestled the doll onto the high shelf that ran the length of the walls of my room alongside the others, and pretty much forgot about her. Perhaps she took offense.

One sunny afternoon a few weeks later, when I was about eight years old, I was upstairs alone in my bedroom, playing with my dollhouse. My attention was always fully absorbed in whatever little drama I was playing out in the miniature rooms with the tiny plastic family that occupied it, but I remember suddenly being pulled from my reverie. I must have heard or seen something in my periphery because I clearly remember looking up to see the Navajo doll floating through the air toward me. It wasn't moving downward as though it had fallen, it traveled at least five feet across the room. I say it was floating because although it was rapidly moving through the air, it was perfectly vertical in flight, not spinning end over end as an object typically does when it is thrown. I was transfixed as I watched it, when suddenly the doll hit me square in the face and fell to the floor. I looked down at it, dumbstruck, and the next minute incensed, as I thought for certain my older brother had come in and, having seen me engrossed in my dollhouse activity, had somehow tossed the doll at me, then hid in the next-door hallway bathroom as a prank. It wouldn't have been the first time he threw something at me for no reason other than "that's what older brothers do."

I stormed into the bathroom, whipping the door open, hoping to smack him with it, expecting to find him ready to burst into laughter at having scared me, but no one was there. I ran downstairs, passing my mother in the living room, and asked her if my brother had just come down ahead of me. To my puzzlement, she said no; he'd been in the kitchen awhile, rummaging in the fridge. I was instantly unnerved – the more I considered it, I realized the doll hadn't simply fallen off the shelf or even moved through the air in the way an object would normally fall – not to mention the fact it had crossed an entire room. I crept back upstairs, gingerly grabbed the doll from where it lay on the floor, and gave it to my mom, who presumably donated it.

Years later, reading Hans Holzer's book *The Ghost Hunter*, I came across a passage that sent chills down to my very toes. He briefly noted that on one of his investigations, he came into contact with "... an Indian doll that falls down from a secure shelf now and then as if someone were throwing it."[1] Reading those words as an adult felt as though a spirit was in the room with me, invisibly staring at me, whispering, "See?" Further research showed me many accounts of these types of dolls and similar claims and finally confirmed for me what I'd always privately concluded about that childhood event – something supernatural had been at play. It had been a nudge from "the Other," waiting to be acknowledged.

Though this odd incident stuck with me as a kid, maybe I'm being stubborn when I say it still really didn't serve as the truly significant moment that I can point to as the definitive start of my interest in ghosts and hauntings. That's my earliest memory of something unexplainable, but I didn't launch into investigating at the age of eight. My interest in ghosts was just a generalized preference, presenting in little ways throughout my childhood. I was a Halloween enthusiast, and I just liked stories that gave me the chills. An avid reader from a young age, I always gravitated toward spooky books by authors like Mary Downing Hahn, who writes ghost stories for kids, and surreptitiously traded copies of *Scary Stories to Tell in the Dark* and *Goosebumps* with my schoolfriends when our teacher wasn't looking. I've always been very close with my cousin, with whom I enjoyed whispering about spooky tales near our family's lakeside cabin, where we congregated each summer. Then, years later, as they came into popularity, I watched paranormal "documentaries" and ghost-hunting shows obsessively, but always my interest was at the level of a casual observer. Ghosts were a steady interest, but never something I integrated into my life in any real way.

When odd experiences happened in my life, I would wonder at the strange goings-on before casually tucking the moments away. I was too busy with pragmatic life. There was the business of growing up, navigating life in an emotionally chaotic childhood, then focusing on school, trying to figure out bits of who I was. After graduating college, I met my husband, and I worked full-time and then was busy raising our children. Looking back now, it's as though throughout my life, I was just always knee-deep in the paranormal and I didn't consciously realize it. I just wasn't ready to *see*.

Then one evening, in a chilling moment on my very first paranormal investigation at Fort Mifflin in Philadelphia, I was. I had a definitive experience that grabbed me by the chin, forcing me to look the paranormal in the figurative eye. Everything changed on a dime.

After that, when I finally dove in, my world opened up. Interestingly, the more I talk with other paranormal investigators, the more it seems this feeling is common, as if something unseen was occasionally attempting to snag our attention, as if it had always been there. Do paranormal investigators join the field because they want to, or are they subtly invited by something unseen?

Diving into the paranormal was an unusual breath of fresh

air – a wake-up call that I had more to give as a passionate, creative, critically thinking individual in the world. In the end, of all things, immersing myself in paranormal research is what saved me from falling into the depths of a dark time in my life.

CHAPTER 2
HELLO, DARKNESS

J umping headfirst into paranormal research was a bright light, a life preserver tossed to me at a time in my life when I desperately needed something to cling to for peace and fulfillment in my life, to find my true self. Depression and anxiety had been eating me alive for years, and though I'd mostly kept these beasts at bay, I was succumbing to a triple threat of unhealed emotional trauma from my early years, stubbornly vicious postpartum depression, and the never-ending exhaustion of young motherhood. An interest in the paranormal had been hovering in the background all my life, a supporting member of the cast, pacing the sidelines but never a key player. The time had come for me to fully acknowledge my interest in it, and when I did, I bloomed.

The past always steps on the heels of the present. In understanding how someone changes, what the bridge between "before" and "after" means, it's important to take a step back to see the full picture of someone's perspective, as much as it can be relayed. Understanding an individual's context is invaluable. I share my private moments and backstory here to show the depth of my personal mental health difficulties and the path motherhood laid before me from the beginning. How cruelly my traitorous brain dragged me into the shadows before I was able to pull myself out again. I think a lot of us in the paranormal field may have similarities in our backstories, if not precisely the same situations; transparency from a peer about mental health struggles can be damn comforting. I think perhaps those of us who have been through any kind of trauma, who have seen and experienced the Dark in one way, are able to withstand Darkness later, or even embrace it. Perhaps we feel a little more comfortable there than others, and we can tackle and digest difficult topics with greater ease.

I have ruminated on the idea that perhaps my interest in the paranormal and macabre was planted into my brain at a young age, growing up alongside a mother who casually and frequently discussed suicide. I have mused that the intense postpartum depression I suffered came on swiftly because it was like muscle memory, my brain had essentially been conditioned for dark thoughts, and it was somehow, in a twisted way, comfortable territory in which to retreat. It was as if the path to a depressed mindset had already been paved and easy to find. As I grew into my maternal instincts, I recognized my propensity for unhealthy dark thoughts, and I changed the narrative within the construct. I remade the path to lead to something Dark, yes, but fascinating and healing instead. In the end, I gathered strength from those who love me, and I made it out alive, albeit with a penchant for the strange and unusual.

Being fascinated by life after death isn't something to be ashamed of, nor does it indicate someone will be the next inspiration for a true crime documentary. Darkness has many faces. Likewise, struggling with dark thoughts toward yourself doesn't make you a bad person. When we feel so low we can't see beyond ourselves, we must dissect *why* we feel the way we do. We need to pull the darkness apart and really look at each jagged, angry, despairing piece and ask, "How did I get here?" And then comes the critical step: finding the way out.

If my story resonates with just one reader who feels *seen*, or someone who judges his- or herself less harshly for having dark thoughts, whether or not he or she is a parent, then I feel vindicated in my vulnerability. Hard days come. They should be expected. Mental health is not a battle won once and forever victorious. It is a process of recognizing the approach of a rough period and what helps. The recovery path that worked for me in the early years of motherhood would come into play later, when I started researching the paranormal.

In the summer of 2014, when I was six months pregnant, I chose to leave my managerial job to transition to the life of a stay-at-home mother. I know it's the norm to hate your job, but I liked mine, and I was sad to leave despite my simultaneous excitement about the new life path I was forging. Actually, I sobbed as I left the building on my final day. Of course, in my time there, I had my typical gripes about work like any employed person does, about hours and fatigue and the like, but I was successful, and I took a lot of pride in my performance. I typically came home feeling I had earned my pay, and that my efforts made a positive impact on the success of my company overall. But after five years or so of climbing the ranks at my company, I'd joyfully become pregnant with our first child – something my husband and I had desperately wanted. Our big-picture plan had always been for me to be a stay-at-home mother, and though it was what I wanted, part of me dreaded leaving the position for which I'd worked so diligently. It also meant I was leaving the majority of my social circle behind. I was excited for more time to myself before the baby came, and looked forward to being there for him once he was born, but my world suddenly looked starkly different from the one I knew.

It was a big transition, suddenly being at home instead heading off to work each day. I can't say I didn't enjoy my newfound freedom at first. A natural introvert in most settings, I had always been comfortable being alone, filling my time with various interests and accomplishing my own to-do lists. But after a couple of weeks, I started to keenly miss my work friends and old routine. I missed feeling useful, and I found myself occasionally briefly second-guessing my choice to be a mother who stayed home. But I'd shake those thoughts off and busy myself preparing for my son's arrival – cleaning and recleaning the nursery, buying wipes and creams and shampoos, and envisioning what he would look like. I'd force myself to daydream about the good parts – baby laughs and how adorably tiny all the clothing was as I folded it, sitting in his nursery. I reassured myself that soon I'd be so busy with my son that I wouldn't have time to feel anything but grateful joy. Right?

The many doctor appointments leading up to your child's birth don't adequately prepare first-time mothers for the assault of emotions that come with new motherhood. There are endless blood tests and anatomy scans, but only a brief mention here and there of the baby blues and postpartum lows. There really should be much greater emphasis and discussion of how hard it is emotionally, and whether you may be prone to full-blown postpartum depression or anxiety, especially given your own family life as a child. If you were raised in an unstable, traumatic, or difficult family situation yourself, or are prone to dark thoughts in the first place, the roller coaster of new motherhood may viciously root these thoughts out and bring them into the light of day. I was going to learn this the hard way.

My due date passed by for five days, as I waited for a sign that my son was ready to join us Earthside. One evening, I felt the sure signs that he was on his way, and along with the physical sensations, I suddenly felt the stirrings of emotions I was not anticipating. It was as though with the start of labor, alongside the inklings of joy at the idea of soon meeting my boy, I couldn't shake the thought that I was about to be permanently "on-the-clock" for the next eighteen years or so. It was about to become real, and though physically, all was going as it should, emotionally, I was starting to panic.

My thoughts took sudden dark turns, and anxiety held the reins. I clearly remember thinking that my newborn son, just by existing, would prove to the world how unfit I would be as a mother. My inevitable failure was about to be seen in broad daylight. I was shocked and appalled by my own inner dialogue. Meanwhile, on the outside, I was telling the doctor, nurses, and even my husband how excited I was. Looking back, recognizing that these cruel, negative thoughts like some variation of imposter syndrome sprang up as soon as labor began, I should have known right then that something was wrong with my mental health. I'd been a walking red flag disguised as a glowing mommy-to-be.

Not for the first time, I wished desperately for a sage elder, a woman who'd been in my shoes, whom I trusted and admired. Someone I trusted to tell me that everything would be OK, to help guide me in how to help myself through this dark cloud. Unfortunately, I just didn't have that person. Not really.

My own mother and I have a difficult relationship. Any mother-daughter relationship is a mercurial thing; growing up, a lot of people told me how lucky I was to have such a wonderful, devoted mother. Yes, she was intermittently the mother I wanted – sometimes she listened to my problems, and we enjoyed movie nights or occasional shopping trips. However, most of the time, we merely operated under the guise of a happy family, concealing that I was actually growing up under the wing of a bipolar mother with alcohol issues. Her mental health struggles meant she talked about committing suicide as casually as deciding whether or not she should run errands that day or the next, and I carried a lot of the emotional load in my house.

My father was always pretty emotionally unattached from our family dynamic, always neutral, as if it wasn't his place to interfere or assist; his dissociated behavior seemed normal to me at the time. My older brother is eight years older than me and has always been my hero. But he was well on his hard-earned way to building his own adult life in the world when it was my turn to be in the thick of it at home with my mother. My brother was (and is) often my sounding board and became my surrogate role model as time went on, but there are many times in life a girl just needs a trusted female mentor.

As a teenager, my family life was difficult to navigate – I needed my mother as much as any teenage girl does, but I often felt the burden of her current emotional state, as if it were mine to regulate. Manic-depressive disorder is a strange beast; my mother excelled at making holidays special and sometimes there were longer periods of clarity in which we'd relax and joke, and things were good. But it was a completely unpredictable roller coaster, depending entirely on her mental health on any given day. Would she skip her meds this week? Will we have dinner together, or will she go to bed at 2 p.m.? Is she going to call my friend from school and yell at her when I come home sad after a hard day at school? We went around and around in a cycle of stifling closeness, leading to horrible screaming matches, followed by predictable apologies, after which the cycle began anew. I felt sympathy for her struggles, I really did, but after years of so many explosive fights and being blamed for problems in her life that had nothing to do with me, I was exhausted. I lived in a state of constant anxiety.

Finding empty beer bottles hidden down the side of her bed against the wall as I looked for the tennis ball to play with our dog opened my eyes that mine was not the average mother my friends were growing up with. Shouldn't the teenager be hiding beer bottles from her mother and not the other way around? I realized that it was not, in fact, normal to tell your daughter, "I wish I had cancer. Then if I died, no one would blame me." It was devastating to hear her say that then; it's devastating to remember it now.

Part of my "normal" included several series of days in my youth when no one had seen nor heard from her in days. We feared the worst each time, but in the end, each time, someone would eventually locate her, and all was well for the moment. We'd all move right along with our lives as if nothing had happened. Each instance wore me down just a little bit more inside, fraying my already-raw teenage psyche to ribbons. But this was my family's "normal." My reality at that time of my life was: if I failed in maintaining my mother, she would finally end her life, and it would be my fault. Consequently, I struggled a great deal with panic disorder and my own dark thoughts throughout high school and my early college days.

I went away to college, and though our relationship continued to struggle, I tested out my new independence living on my own. After some hiccups in finding my way, I started to feel lighter. Month by month, I tried to rescind the obligation of being my mother's keeper, little by little. I was a burgeoning adult in the world, and it was time I created some protective boundaries for myself. The physical distance of being away at school made it easier to separate emotionally and start forging my own path. I was proud of myself for stepping out from under the burdens of my youth, but as an adult, my chaotic relationship with my mother left me with a gaping hole where a valued role model should have been.

All things considered, it is unsurprising that I suffered horribly from postpartum depression with my firstborn. I should have known that I was headed for a calamity at this huge turning point in my life. I was dealing with suddenly leaving my job and being isolated at home, with a lack of the proverbial "village" of help, topped off with a history of mental illness in my family. Becoming a mother for the first time is enough to topple the most stalwart of women. Postpartum depression is sneaky and makes you feel such shame at feeling anything but joy and gratefulness. You never expect it to come, even when the dreadful stars aligned for it to arise. "That won't happen to me. I wanted this," you say to yourself, brushing it off.

When my son was born, I truly was overjoyed to have an easy birth to a healthy little boy. I marveled at his tininess and the fact that he wanted me above all others. That my touch literally soothed his raging cries when I first held him. But always, *always* in the back of my mind or heart, or both, I thought I would fail. My brain told me my little boy didn't realize yet what a selfish mother I would be, or how I wouldn't know how to help him. I wish I could go back in time and give myself a hug.

Of course, I kept these negative thoughts private, as I tried to be the portrait of a blissful new mother. Even the night my son was born, when my husband left the hospital for the night at my urging to get some proper sleep in our bed at home, I fell apart. I'd told him to go, and I meant it. He didn't want to leave, but I convinced him he needed rest to support me the next day, and that I was OK. About ten minutes after he left, the nurses took my baby boy to the nursery at my request, and I carefully plodded to my little private washroom, where my emotions welled up to a crescendo and the dam burst. I could not help but start sobbing uncontrollably. It was the kind of crying that racks your body with shuddering gasps. I was mortified that I didn't realize in my state how loud I was, that my doctor heard me from the hallway and quietly knocked on my door.

"Mallory, are you OK?"

"Oh... yes... sorry... I'm fine."

Ahh, yes. The classic reply. I'm fine. Nothing about my mental health that night was fine.

My doctor coaxed me out of the washroom and sat on my bed with me. She spoke quietly about the tidal wave of emotion that naturally comes after birth, and I nodded and thanked her. She asked the nurses to bring me some sleeping medicine. A few minutes later it was brought to me and placed on my bedside table; I flushed it down the toilet after my nurse left the room. My anxiety at failing as a mother had already sunk its terrible claws into the places of my brain that whispered venomous lies to me – "If you take that, you'll be asleep when the baby needs you... if you do manage to wake up, you'll be so tired holding him that you'll drop him on his head, and he'll be dead before you even leave the hospital." Things I'd never utter to my worst enemy.

Some women slide into motherhood like a duck to water; others rage and panic and fret on their way to the pond, even when they want to swim. The path of motherhood is different for everyone, but it changes you so that you can easily find yourself and your thoughts unrecognizable in a very short amount of time. To be clear, I'm not so blind as to entirely blame my mother or my upbringing for my own mental health issues; sudden and vicious postpartum depression can strike any new mother, to varying degrees, at different times in the journey. It's so much more common than is divulged, the shame that accompanies it often keeping its victims silent. My days were lonely and I was ashamed that I didn't feel the boundless joy I had been expecting. Late nights and long sleep-deprived months steeped in dark thoughts worm their way inside and change core things about who you are and how you react to the world. In the late hours of the sleepless night, our minds can all go to some dark places. There were times when my son was a few weeks old when my inner voice horrified me by sounding exactly like my mother when she ideated suicide.

CHAPTER 3

LITTLE RECOVERIES,
AGAIN AND AGAIN

I did not want to be someone who casually considered suicide as a viable option. Not ever. The passionate desire to not be that person helped me power through the worst of the dark thoughts long enough for my new routine to settle in. I muddled through at the beginning, my equally groggy husband by my side. As time went on and my son slept more, so did I, and though the shame and despair lost their fierce edges, they transformed into more of a constant numb fog that clung to me. I wasn't truly *there*; I was going through the motions like an automaton. I loved my baby, but I knew I was missing out on really appreciating the joy of new motherhood. Something had to change.

After many childhood years of seeing my mother on every imaginable array of medicines, I felt strongly (probably stubbornly) that medication wasn't right for me. However, I was desperate for relief, and logically, I knew that medication had been the key to the recovery of countless others, despite my personal aversion. So at my doctor's urging, I agreed to trying it for a few weeks. Unfortunately, the intense side effects I experienced merely amplified my problems to unbearable levels. After multiple nights of insomnia followed by hours of vomiting left me barely able to physically function, I couldn't take it anymore. While prescribed medicine from a trusted doctor is absolutely the right path for many, I knew it wasn't a fit for me. I gave it a chance, but I knew on some personal level that it wasn't the right fit. I needed to distance myself from the memory of seeing medications strewn on the bathroom counter. Perhaps I was trying to intellectualize my way out, but I wanted a behavioral and holistic option to pull myself through. It was a matter of foolish pride, mixed with a little shame, but I wanted to figure it out myself. Eventually, I realized that what I truly needed was to feel more like myself again, and not just my baby's mother. Of utmost importance in my recovery was going to be championing my sense of individuality by enriching my time with interests beyond my child. I needed to feel like a whole person again, not just "Mommy."

I started throwing myself into anything I ever found interesting. At that time in my life, while I binged ghost shows and casually read about paranormal theories, it just hadn't yet occurred to me that actually investigating the paranormal was an option I could pursue. So, though I loved ghosts and "spooky stuff," it wasn't one of the hobbies I turned to then. I opened an Etsy storefront and sold handmade gifts. I trained for local 5K races and lost the baby weight. I dabbled in this and that until I felt like I had more than just my newborn's needs occupying my mind twenty-four seven. Hobbies initially meant as distraction started to give me a temporary sense of self-worth again. It was incredibly helpful to energetically pursue my interests, and my efforts started to lift the haze of hopelessness and self-doubt.

Soon I felt stronger and therefore humble enough to recognize that I needed more help. I let myself open up and ask for help where I could; my good friends and my mother-in-law were Godsends. I took care of myself and acknowledged my emotions as they came. I reached out to other local mothers, and though that never was exactly the right social fit ("Do you like ghosts?" isn't an ideal typical icebreaker question at Mommy & Me groups, I've found), I felt hopeful again and started to truly enjoy my wondrous little boy. Knowing I could still be an individual while also being a mother made a huge difference to me. I started to heal. I started to feel OK again. I was grateful for that simple progress, compared to those early days.

My son grew into such a wonderful little boy, and I found little ways to hoist myself further up, day after day. My husband and I remained strong for and with each other, and by the time my son was three and obviously the smartest, sweetest child there ever was, we were overjoyed to welcome our daughter into the world. I had intense trepidation in the last months of my pregnancy with her: "Would all those negative, cruel feelings I'd chased away return?" But happily, I felt overwhelmingly relieved when I felt only joy and hope in the first hours and days of her life. A few months down the road, when sleepless nights piled up, hints of those old dark feelings tried to emerge in the wee hours of the night, or when my daughter would cry for hours on end with no respite, but I was better prepared this time around, having gone through the trenches of infancy and toddlerhood once before. My mental health toolkit was already assembled, and though it was still work reaching back into it, I felt stronger in this bout. I knew that I needed to ask for help, and to keep my boundaries firm. I was proud of staying afloat and present, though it certainly was another world having two children to look after.

Time went by, and while I kept up with my hobbies, mostly I was "Mom," and that was actually OK. I was better at it than I thought I'd be (most days), and as a child of the unexpected peaks and valleys of emotional trauma, I did not mind steering a home of routine and daily rhythms, both for myself and my family. But OK is no way to live long term, not for me.

"Gratitude unlocks the fullness of life," as Mother Theresa said, and I like to think that I am grateful on a daily basis. And though I knew, by being constantly reminded by social media posts and well-meaning elderly women in Target, that this time would "go too fast" and I should "treasure every moment," I needed a little more; I *was* a little more. These sentiments from little old ladies with too-bright lipstick had me growing a seed of worry, nagging concerns about myself: Will my kids want to hang out with me when they are adults? Who would I be once these treasured days were a little less grueling? Was I inadvertently following the same familiar path I'd been working so hard to avoid?

I tucked these worries away as they came, distracted with the demands of daily life. A few years into diapers and endless bowls of fish-shaped crackers (and finding said crackers in every single furniture crevice), on very little sleep, trying to make time for *me*, plus managing my relationships and life in general – it's no wonder the smooth veneer of my well-oiled, blissfully predictable routine started to develop a crack here and there. (I still don't comprehend how mothers of more than two do it.) Occasionally, random pangs of intensely low feelings hit me, catching me off guard. Despite my best efforts and genuinely enjoying *most* facets of my life, one day, the acidic voice in my head whispered, "All you are is a mother. And you're not very good at it."

But this time, *this time*, I said back to the Dark voice: "Oh no you don't. Not this time."

I've always wanted to break the cycle of mothering under the haze of depression, without low confidence weighing me down. I wanted to thrive and to be a fulfilled, honest, genuinely happy role model for my children, and I was willing to fight for it. I wanted them to see me quick to smile and easy to get excited about things. I just didn't realize that embracing the weird parts of myself would be the key to feeling like the best version of me. It was time to find a true passion, and I needed to really step outside my comfort zone to do so. While I appreciated the interests that helped me through postpartum feelings, there were none I dreamed about at night, none I passionately looked forward to each day. Arts and crafts had lost their luster, and my bookshelves sagged with copy after copy of books I'd read. This time, as I cast my net afresh, something new, yet also familiar, caught my eye. I was about to finally take a step towards my interest in the paranormal by way of a local event I saw online.

CHAPTER 4

FIRST TASTE OF THE PARANORMAL

In the summer of 2019, Pennhurst State School, which is a mere ten minutes from my house, announced they were hosting a huge paranormal convention event, with guest speakers I'd never hoped to have the chance to meet. I barely hesitated before snapping up tickets, and I couldn't wait for the day to arrive.

On July 24, 2019, the sun blazed down on the grounds of Pennhurst State School, scorching the air to a humid 100°F. I strolled through the stifling vendor area, browsing macabre items for sale, when suddenly I turned a corner. At the far end of the tent, I saw paranormal personalities I'd seen over and over again on my favorite TV shows. I took a breath and joined the throngs of people milling around them. When I arrived at the front of the line, to chat with them and take some photos, the elation I felt was mildly embarrassing, even to myself. My son, then four years old, had even drawn a portrait of one of them as a gift, which was enthusiastically accepted and appreciated – one of the highlights of that day.

Later, I sat in the lecture tent, sweat dripping down my

temples, completely rapt, listening to the speakers discuss paranormal investigation theories and tactics nonchalantly, as if everyone in the audience had also done it, or should. I looked around, noticing shirts declaring various paranormal teams and haunted locations. I realized that in this crowd, not having investigated yet, I was the odd woman out. I was fascinated. These were people with their own figurative freak flags, and their flags matched mine. It was right then that the first seed of an idea was sown in my brain – I could actually go on paranormal investigations too. Myself.

Cue 2020. What is there even left to say? It stopped us all in our tracks; plans and ideas frozen in time as we were all forced to pause and focus inward. In March 2020, in the early stages of quarantine, I felt like I needed to really step up my game and keep spirits high. I felt it was my mission to ensure my children knew that they were safe and things would be OK. I wanted to rise to the challenge. We were extremely lucky in our circumstances, we were healthy, staying home was doable, if chaotic, and we stayed optimistic.

So many mornings that spring had me, like so many mothers across the globe, sitting in my kitchen with my kindergartner, trying to corral him into finishing his sight word worksheets while begging my three-year-old to keep her diaper on while emphatically whisper-yelling, "Everyone try to be super quiet because Daddy has a work call!" in his home office. But quarantine just kept going, and the world was so angry, and eventually, more and more parts of life were canceled, and Covid news was inescapable. Toddlers had to learn to wear masks, and you couldn't find chicken or toilet paper anywhere; it's safe to say we all lost our minds at least a little bit, as the walls pushed in. I was still determined to make my kids feel safe, but that was a tough period for all of us. An understatement, I think.

Insert here the obligatory – yet also sincere – sentiment of gratitude for my life situation and family, even after my private battles for my sanity in the early years of my children's lives. I was one of those moms who actually enjoyed the mandatory extra time with my favorite people. But motherhood is filled to the brim with hypocritical, contradictory emotions. While I loved the quality time we were getting, after three months at home, the sensation of feeling eroded as an individual was returning, bit by bit. I was almost six years into motherhood, three of those years with two in tow, and I just hadn't done much but be there for them. No matter how many self-care articles pop up online, it's expected, and often required, that mothers give up big chunks of themselves. Kids need and need and need, and while we're happy and proud to have that responsibility, at the end of the day, we are burnt to a crisp. I was determined to reclaim myself while still giving my children a stable and happy home. I was ready to charge ahead from the point where Covid had thwarted my plans for growth.

Happily, around the same time that quarantine restrictions were easing, I looked around and, to my astonishment, realized that my kids were growing up just enough that I had a (very little) bit more freedom to look into paranormal investigation opportunities, which required my being out of the house. My kids were old enough that it was less of a hardship to toss them both on my husband for a night, or ask my mother-in-law to stop by. I thought back to how I'd felt sitting in that tent at Pennhurst the summer prior and knew I wanted to try a ghost hunt. It seemed things in my life were aligned so that I was ready to explore my interest in the paranormal. It wasn't until late summer 2020 that an opportunity popped up online to attend a public overnight investigation at Fort Mifflin in Philadelphia.

CHAPTER 5

THE BEGINNING: FORT MIFFLIN

L iving just outside Philadelphia has me happily situated near plenty of historically significant locations. Fort Mifflin, one such site, is located in an area called Mud Island on the Delaware River, adjacent to Philadelphia proper. I had never been there before, but a quick dive into its history told me the fort had been captured in 1777 by the British Army as part of their conquest of Philadelphia in the Revolutionary War. Once back under U.S. control, it served as officers' quarters, training grounds for the militia, as well as the local commandant's home. Prisoners during the Civil War were held in the casemates, arched prison cells buried partly underground.[2] A fully underground cell was recently discovered by a groundskeeper after being mysteriously buried for many years. The fort was used to store ammunition for World Wars I and II before finally being decommissioned in 1962. It is currently used for historical reenactments, history tours, and paranormal investigations like the one I had seen advertised.

Something inside me perked up, and my brain fizzed with excitement as I read about the chance to attend a real investigation, let alone at a site I had seen featured on my favorite spooky TV shows. Excited as I was, I wasn't confident enough to go traipsing into the dark on my own right out of the gate, so I reached out to a friend, another mother who I assumed was feeling as cooped up as I was. Indeed, she jumped at the chance to get out as quickly as I was keen to, and plans were set. Covid ended up being the catalyst I needed to take the next step in my paranormal journey. I just didn't realize how much my life would change by purchasing that ticket.

FORT MIFFLIN, ONE MONTH LATER

We broke off from the rest of the group and walked down the stone path of the casemate hallway, the low, curved ceiling above us dully reflecting the glow from the lanterns they had lit to set the mood. A young tour guide dressed in period military clothes had been skittishly taking us from site to site throughout the fort all evening, and though it had been fun and interesting, the overall creepy factor had been lower than I'd anticipated; it was nice to get away on our own and explore one of the most notoriously haunted sections of the fort unaccompanied.

I'd read, "You have to check out casemate 5!" over and over on ghost-hunting websites and in articles leading up to that night, so I figured we should go have a look before the night's public investigation wrapped up and we had to head home. It was my first paranormal investigation ever, and I loved every minute of it, even though most of it had been quiet. Nothing had happened, really, all night in the rest of the fort – some interesting sensations of chills at the back of my neck here and there, enough to call it a fun adventure, out trying something new in a year where most other public events had been canceled. By this point, my friend and I were over the nerves we had felt upon arriving hours earlier, and we were more casual about wandering into the dark. Casemate 5 was at the end of the shadowed corridor, and we shined our phone flashlights into each dark cell as we passed them. We entered the final casemate, the wooden benches stretching out in front of us into the gloom of the far end of the chamber. It was cold and vaguely damp, an uncomfortable space for anyone to be in for long. A cold fireplace hearth stood behind us to the right. Feeling bold, I stepped up and knocked on the bench in front of me, foolishly excited to playact a scene I'd seen so many times on television shows I'd watched through the years.

"Hello," I said to the air. "If anyone is in here with us, can you knock back like this?" This would be, unknown to me at the time, the first time of many, many times I sent a question into the darkness, hoping for a ghostly response. As it was, at that moment, I felt very silly.

Knock, knock. I rapped on the bench.

Silence.

My friend and I murmured to each other about how cold the casemate was, how dismal. A few moments later, she wandered up the middle path between the rows of benches.

I asked, "Is there anyone here with us?"

Silence.

A beat or two of quiet, then with her back to me, my friend asked, "Do you want us to leave?"

Immediately, to my right, a desperate male voice: "NO."

My heart froze for a second. My friend spun quietly on her heel, her wide eyes mirroring my own as she gazed in the direction of the disembodied voice, while goosebumps suddenly covered my body.

"That was a 'no,'" she whispered.

I nodded, completely shocked and ready to bolt from the room.

"Yes. Yes, that was. From right... there." I pointed to a completely empty space next to me.

W hen the event had begun hours earlier, I fangirled at seeing a K2 meter in real life. I had been cordoned off into a small group with my friend and a stranger throughout the evening and led to various sites within the fort by a member of a local paranormal team. We changed to new spots in the fort every hour or so. In the first session, we went to the Commandant's House. We were instructed that it was OK to move beyond the "no admittance" ropes and explore the crumbling brick foundation within, a thrill in itself. The other investigators laid down pieces of equipment, and I was totally giddy. This was legitimately the first time I had seen this equipment with my own eyes instead of on a screen after so many years of bingeing "ghost shows." I was even excited to sit in the dark, in the quiet. I remember thinking, as I sat in the Officer's Quarters in the third hour of the event, that it had been a great night in my book, just to try this for the first time. I felt refreshed already and was casually wondering to myself when I might be able to do this again. Then, at the tail end of the night, after we were told we could spend the last hour visiting whichever location in the fort we hadn't gone to yet, we visited casemate 5, and I was forever changed by that disembodied voice.

After we heard the voice, in all honesty, I pulled a move right out of *Scooby Doo* and ran for the door, forever to my chagrin – a classic rookie move I still get teased about, and rightfully so. My friend half mocking/half chastising told me to get back in there, where she still stood, rooted to her original spot. I laughed at my body's automatic flight response and slowly made my way back into the room, apologizing aloud to the spirit for leaving when he'd literally just said he wanted us to stay. My friend came to me, and we stood shoulder to shoulder, facing the room. I fumbled for the phone in my pocket and began recording the empty room in front of us. Nothing happened for a few moments, so I clicked my camera off.

We stood in the silence, absolutely still, hoping to hear something more. I felt a pressure building. Suddenly, I heard a faint buzzing sound like a giant bumblebee approaching. As the sound grew in volume as it got closer, something buzzed past my left ear, and the hair on that side flipped away from my face, as if a phantom hand had roughly brushed it away. I gasped and wheeled around, using my phone for light, but saw nothing, no ghost hand nor behemoth insect speeding away. My friend hadn't heard or felt anything, but we both fled the room at that point, seeking out the other investigators we had met to excitedly relay what we had experienced.

A small group gathered around us just outside the main casemates entrance as we explained what had just occurred. They insisted we go back in. I was feeling afraid now, and the feeling only intensified when one of the group leaders closed the door to the casemate behind us. We were locked in with whatever was there. The leader from the other group walked into the room, putting pieces of equipment on six of the wooden benches and calling out to the spirit aggressively. He'd been to the fort before and insisted he knew the spirit to be a negative entity. Later, I'd look back and cringe at his abrasive style, but in the moment, I was scared and numbly watched things unfold.

As he called out derogatory names to the spirit, challenging him to make himself known, a tangible cold chill began to creep through the room. The room was dark, damp, and prone to unpleasantness already, but this concentration of cold was a sentient thing. It seemed to weave around us, closely inspecting each of us in turn. I felt it come close and back away a few times, until at one point I felt this patch of cold roll uncomfortably close up the front of my body. When it felt like it started to caress my chin, I reeled backward and lunged behind an acquaintance I'd met that night. At that moment, literally every piece of equipment that the leader had placed down began to go off. The darkness of the room was suddenly illuminated by a strobe light effect of flickering lights of the proximity and EMF equipment and the ringing of alarms from other pieces. The beeps echoing off the arched walls mixed with our shouts of surprise. The lights shone on the faces of those around me, throwing their expressions into sharp relief. The cold still lingered. I have no shame when I say I felt terror in that moment. But I felt exhilaration too. Looking back, now owning some of these pieces of equipment myself and having used them in many investigations, I realize how rare that frenzy of activity was. It still sends shivers down my arms when I recall that night.

I was hooked. It was almost as though the Other had given it all in that moment, as though some ghostly voice was figuratively crying out, "Finally!" as I let my enthusiasm free. Where I may have once run from these experiences or set them aside as an unusual passing moment, I could no longer ignore the pull of the paranormal; I now turned toward it and craved more. This was the missing piece of my own puzzle I'd been searching for.

CHAPTER 6

AWKWARDLY REPEAT AFTER ME: "I'M A PARANORMAL INVESTIGATOR"

I t feels as though the other side of the veil is forever watching the living, searching for those who will hear its call, feel its gentle touch. I think throughout my life, the Unseen had been testing me, checking to see if I was ready for more, to explore and connect with *more*. With so many skeptics-at-heart in the world, are we believers chosen? Are we naturally inclined to observe more of what the paranormal world has to show us? Can we train our intuitive senses to be better – to see, feel, smell, and taste more than the mundane of the everyday? While I view my experiences through a skeptical lens, looking for the reasonable answers where I can, I cannot help but return time and again to the idea that some of us are predisposed and then molded by preference and repeated exposure to be "successful" paranormal researchers.

When I was a kid, every so often, I would experience a sudden rising of the hairs on my arm in a quiet room, an unexpected scent of perfume of a deceased relative wafting past as I read my book, or even the sense of being watched by something when I was alone. These sensations have only increased as I have opened myself fully to the possibility of such things; I have on occasion heard an unfamiliar child's voice call out, "Mommy!" when my children are both fast asleep, or caught an unusual shadow passing through the hallway out of the corner of my eye.

~

After everything that happened at Fort Mifflin, it wasn't long before I was filling my schedule as much as I reasonably could with investigations. I felt a wild thrill at what I had experienced, and I knew in my bones that devoting time to this field was the right call for me. I began reading more about paranormal theories and communication techniques and finding accounts of local haunted locations within driving distance. Some ideas were wholly new to me; some made me feel vindicated in my standing viewpoints. (Some made me slack-jawed with just how far some investigators have pursued various rabbit holes.)

I felt as though I wasn't only reaping the satisfaction of enriching my days with fresh ideas and experiences, but I sensed that perhaps in the long run, I would find a sense of belonging and community if I leaned into this. As a stay-at-home mother, my usual days could be lonely and nearly void of adult interaction, and I'd hoped my new hobby would steer me in the direction of like-minded women with whom I enjoyed chatting, even it was just via social media.

I'd always had a hard time making lasting friendships apart from a very special few individuals and my husband. I've just always felt a little clumsy socially. When I was younger, I was often distracted by my home life, and my supremely awkward teenage years didn't help. I loved the idea of a big group of people who would always have my back, but I never quite found my crowd. In college, I made some lifelong friends, the ones who nowadays sometimes happen to call me the instant I'm thinking of dialing their number. These are the kinds of special friends you hold tight to, who prove you don't always need a huge social circle. But it's still nice to meet new people, so sometimes it's frustrating trying to do so as an introverted adult with a busy schedule. It's difficult to manage the logistics of grabbing a cocktail with my friend of twenty plus years, let alone someone new. Not to mention, when I meet another mom at a PTA meeting, in my head I'm usually chanting, "Don't talk about ghosts, don't talk about ghosts..." I like to unveil my quirks bit by bit, thank you.

So while new friendship potential was vaguely on my radar, my predominant "why" at the time I started investigation was to physically be in the field – no longer on the sidelines. If the world really did have incredible spooky secrets to tell, I wanted to be there, seeking them out. My feelings of trudging through the day-to-day feeling like a shell of a person evaporated in the thrill of the paranormal and the possibilities ahead.

CHAPTER 7

THE COST OF PARANORMAL INVESTIGATING

I longed to travel the country to set my feet inside some of the most famously haunted spots across America. My dream locations included Waverly Hills Sanitorium in Kentucky, The Stanley Hotel in Colorado, the Omni Mount Washington Resort in New Hampshire, and more. I enjoyed exploring my local area with a fresh perspective, but I longed to visit some of the "big locations." However, I was quick to understand the many warnings people in the field lobbed at me about how expensive this hobby could be. My destination wish list was far longer than any of my resources. There are many moving parts to consider when endeavoring to talk to ghosts, namely those of time, energy, and financial costs.

My time has been at a premium since the day my son was born. Any mother feels this constraint. Then when my daughter was born, my free time generously included walking around the car to the driver's seat after buckling both kids into their car seats. Yes, they were older by the time I was investigating in earnest, but as previously mentioned, I did not and do not have the proverbial "village" of help around me. I don't have a nanny or multiple babysitters on which to call. If I have an obligation or opportunity that requires my children to be elsewhere, my husband needs to amend his work schedule, or on occasion, I ask my mother-in-law, who lives two hours away, for help. My mother-in-law is an incredibly kind and trustworthy support, but it's not her job to be at my beck and call, and my husband accommodates my interest as much as he can before he too feels the stifling walls of parenthood creep in. Some mothers can schedule spa days or weekend trips with friends at the drop of a hat, and kudos to them, but I don't think I'm alone in the situation, both logistically and financially, when I admit I can't do that very easily.

If I sound crabby and jealous, I suppose that's partially true. I'm genuinely happy for those with an easier go at motherhood, because it's a hard enough gig in any scenario, and I know others have it much harder than me. Mostly I share this gripe because I've seen how the realities of motherhood are so often overlooked in the paranormal field. If a mother has to decline an invitation to a ghost hunt, it is so often mistaken as a lack of interest, when in reality it is usually just a matter of timing and logistics. Investigations are generally on weekend evenings, which cut short quality family time together.

In my home, like many families with school-age kids, Monday through Friday afternoon separates us all with work, school, sports schedules, and life's many responsibilities. Weekend time is precious. Before I started investigating, rarely had my husband and I argued about anything, really; accommodating a new time-consuming hobby tested our mettle on more than one occasion. We have learned to find balance, and I've had to cut back on my nights away. At the beginning, I was obsessed with packing my schedule to the brim, and I have had to temper my interest so that it fit our family life in a more long-term way. I have learned to be OK with saying no sometimes, to missing out on an interesting investigation in favor of time with my family. If it's a location or group of investigators that I really feel pulled toward, we find a way to make it work so I can attend. However, even if an investigation fits my schedule, aligning multiple schedules of fellow investigators can seem like a full-time job. Everyone needs to be devoted to making it work, or the logistics quickly become overwhelming.

Regarding my scant energy, feel free to reference my literally falling asleep during one of the creepiest sessions of an investigation I've ever witnessed, nestled into the dilapidated couch of a haunted ex-brothel. The ghostly voices and creepy laughter drifting from a piece of equipment called a Phasmabox on the table in front of me may as well have been a lullaby. I struggled to keep my eyes open. Granted, I had, that night, experienced some serious activity on location – including seeing an apparition for the first time, so this mom was a bit worn out. I've tried to excuse my exhaustion as the spirits using up my energy for their manifestations (more on that later), but I am open to the idea that I. Was. Tired. Realistically, how many mothers can reach 3 in the morning feeling sprightly and engaged, especially when the hours-long drive home leaves at 7 a.m.? It's exhaustion at its finest. Like so many fellow investigators, I've become a connoisseur of energy drinks and know precisely at what hour to drink them for the best results for the night ahead. Yes, getting even *less* sleep: another check in the column of reasons why paranormal investigation is an unusual hobby for mothers of young children.

Money matters are probably the most impeding factor to booking investigation evenings for many people, no matter the financial standing of a household. Tickets to a public investigation are usually around the $100 mark, more so if a "paranormal celebrity" is in attendance or it is a prominent location.

The cost of renting a location privately can be downright obscene.

This is not to mention the cost of travel, accommodations if you can't sleep on-site, or the big one: equipment. Equipment can be quite the polarizing subject in itself; diehards often fall on either side of the battle between tech versus intuition. Happily, I have noticed a trend toward a blending of the two, which is my preferred style. In short, when you have finally reached your haunted destination, you don't want to spend the majority of your time staring at a tiny illuminated screen or hoping for a beep from a piece of $400 proximity equipment, when you could be sitting quietly, ears pricked for an unexplainable sound or voice, or even the pressure of an unseen touch. It's nice to have evidence to review and examine later, but being in the moment is paramount. It's all about balance.

CHAPTER 8

A HOT TAKE ON PARANORMAL EQUIPMENT

There are many ever-evolving pieces of equipment that investigators use – rarely have I seen such a resourceful inventor as a paranormal researcher. For the purposes of basic understanding, paranormal equipment generally falls under the heading of one of the following: pieces that attempt to acknowledge physical proximity of spirit, pieces that record audio or lend an audible "voice" to spirit, and pieces that record video, with many nuances in between. More are developed every day. None have been proven to absolutely confirm the existence of ghosts, but many have offered fascinating correlational data.

There is a unique branch of paranormal equipment that attempts to enhance your experience in the moment. While some pieces like the parabolic microphone literally enhance the audio in your immediate environment, some are thought to help the user tune into their "inner eye" to enhance the experience psychically. These include tools such as tarot cards or dowsing rods (which are handheld bars that some think may be moved by spirits). Some tech setups become quite complex, ranging from such things as a Farraday cage (in very simple terms: a metal barrier to block all outside radio frequencies, reducing external contamination) all the way to constructing a complex sensory-deprivation setup in which an investigator floats blindfolded in a tub of salt water. (Yes, like on *Stranger Things*.)

Recently, less daunting, more portable devices in the same vein have been rising in popularity. This would include devices like the "Dream Machine," in which you are supposedly lulled into a hypnotic state by staring into a spinning cylinder with rapidly flashing lights. The idea is that in this state, while you are visually distracted by a repetitive pattern, you are more likely to be open to stimuli received psychically (i.e., you can hear or sense a ghost's message more clearly).

Some common proximity-sensing pieces include the REM-Pod, which is usually a short, softball-sized cylinder that emits its own invisible electromagnetic field (EMF), reaching about three inches or so around itself. If that field is interrupted, lights and sound indicate that something is nearby. There are also music box devices that shoot an infrared (IR) beam in one direction, playing a chilling tune if the IR beam is disrupted. A most entertainingly named piece, the "cat ball," is literally a ball toy originally manufactured for use by cats. If it is nudged with enough force, it glows flashing colors, indicating it has been disturbed. (And "cat balls" are just so good for endless laughs.) There are temperature-fluctuation alert systems, to offer quantitative measurements of a "cold spot" or even the bodily form of an apparition on-screen, presumably colder or warmer than the surrounding environment. There are SLS cameras, which attempt to use digital depth-of-field sensors in cameras to map out humanoid forms unseen by the naked eye. Some devices like the Geophone attempt to measure footsteps or detectable vibration. There are K2 and Mel Meters to

MAKING FRIENDS WITH GHOSTS

measure EMF fluctuations, with varying accuracy. (It is important to note that the Earth itself has a natural EMF field, which fluctuates occasionally. These natural fluctuations can influence any EMF device at random.)

Some devices attempt to give a voice to nearby spirits, in one way or another. There are portable devices meant to decipher radio wave sounds or even offer prerecorded voice banks for spirits to manipulate, with wavering credibility. The popular Spirit Box (especially model SB-7), designed by Gary Galka, rapidly scans radio frequencies and is thought to be an easy conduit for a spirit to manipulate and deliver a message. Somewhat similarly, there are smartphone apps that attempt to use digital dictionaries to match up nearby EMF fluctuations to correlate with words or phrases the spirit supposedly wants to relay. There are eBay battles over certain brands and models of digital audio recorders. There is even a compact computer device called an *Ovilus*, developed by Bill Chappell, which attempts to translate electronic signals into text responses from a preloaded dictionary. These devices in particular can cost upwards of $400 apiece. It's easy to understand how some investigators might want the flashy pieces just for the perceived clout of owning them rather than their true belief in their use in talking with the dead. Then again, it really comes down to personal preference and what you truly feel helps you connect. There are many ways to investigate a haunted location.

Diving into tech and what to buy can be absolutely overwhelming. The good news is that most investigators will tell a greenhorn that almost all tech is like icing on an already-sweet cake: unnecessary (and often distracting). All you truly need is patient attention, a flashlight, and maybe your phone camera, a video camera, or a digital audio recorder. There's no need to bog yourself down with (or drain your bank account for)

MALLORY CYWINSKI

equipment; the most important things to bring to an investigation are a calm demeanor, a level head, and an open mind. Let a location speak to you. If the tech syncs up with a gut feeling, or you receive repetitive responses, or you catch a voice that means something to you in that context, you've hit the jackpot. If you go in with the goal of capturing that elusive piece of evidence with aims to convince a staunch skeptic, you're missing the point of the endeavor. No one piece of tech has ever been shown to prove the absolute existence of a ghost; that may never be possible. We are all working with what we have: hunches, common sense, and a little blind hope.

At the beginning, as I navigated through scheduling investigation weekends and my confidence grew, I picked up a few basic investigation pieces, keeping things simple and relatively affordable. If my skeptic-to-the-bone husband is reading this, may he happily note that I did not purchase the coffin-shaped $450 proximity music box that caught my attention at the paranormal convention I attended last year.

CHAPTER 9

JOINING THE PARACOMMUNITY

A few months into actively investigating, the friend I dragged to Fort Mifflin and I formed our own paranormal team, just us two. Though we were never particularly close friends before our paranormal adventures apart from attending some literary events together and sharing some laughs, we'd known each other through our husbands for over a decade and were both eager to continue investigating after our incredible experience in casemate 5. We realized we wanted to join this community and keep investigating, but as mothers, we needed to do it in a way where we could hold the reins in balancing our new passion and the needs of our family lives. In the first years, we relied on each other for confidence in investigation settings and backup for evidence review and theory discussion. The road trips, the joint experiences, the other friendships we made, and the deep conversations were priceless.

However, a few years into forming our team, even though we were getting invited to events together and to be guests on podcasts, behind the scenes, our friendship was suffering. We each felt comfortable in the community on our own by that point, and the unexpected stressors of trying to be a united front while being such different women with diverging styles and perspectives was a continual source of strife. So as bickering became more and more frequent, we decided to hit the brakes on the team to safeguard our actual friendship. We disbanded on good terms and continued our paranormal adventures as solo investigators. In the end, it was the right move, and we were grateful to realize we could still support each other and even still investigate together.

When we first began being involved in the paranormal community, I was quick to stake out branding across social media accounts to document our adventures. I wasn't sure what I had in mind long term, but I wanted to establish my little corner of it all. Though our follower numbers didn't grow like wildfire, what mattered was that I felt like I found a solid spot in a community that didn't judge my weirdness. As a stay-at-home mother with aforementioned very little free time to make new friends, I have truly enjoyed connecting and sharing ideas with others in the field. Where I would once sometimes go a full, busy day without speaking to another adult apart from my husband as I raised my babies, I now could take a minute here and there during the day to talk with paranormal friends all around the world from my couch. Friendly messages and shared excitement over various paranormal ideas were so special to me then and still are to this day. Conversations over weeks and months led to multiple collaborations and real friendships I never would have had if I hadn't been bold enough to pursue this odd hobby in the first place.

CHAPTER 10

NOTES ON FEAR

A question I am asked time and again by those outside the field is "Aren't you afraid?" The answer is easy. Hell yes I am. I'm a paranormal investigator, but sleeping alone in a room in a haunted house? No, thank you. Part of the pull of the paranormal is trying to distill all-out fear down to the level of a "desired thrill." Some people queue up to sign waivers and enter intense fake haunted houses at Halloween; some people have BDSM sex; some skydive. A level of (perceived) controlled fear is somehow, for some of us, a spike of pleasure rooted in the fascination of experiencing something visceral, in the moment. It's the idea that you were there, boots on the ground, doing the work, in the action. Part of you longs to be afraid, just a little bit. Circling back to my personal paranormal journey and its jolt to my day-to-day routine, a little fear by way of ghosts was just the spark I desired, apparently.

We've all been subjected to not only horror movies with murderous ghosts, but a recent onslaught of paranormal entertainment television shows, which are highly dramatized and, in many cases, fabricated to seem more action-packed than real investigations. I am a hardcore fan of some of these shows myself, but I realize that real investigations are not like what you see on TV. We've all been ingesting these shows featuring decaying buildings with rumors of Satanic cult gatherings and disembodied screams every few minutes. We've watched episode after episode of full-grown men yelling in terror as they run from a "demon who just tried to choke them." Then, as you head to your first investigation, you might be *expecting* a night of stark terror ahead. Yes, often the wallpaper *is* peeling, and there is dust an inch thick along the floors, but your time is most likely to be spent squatting on a dirty folding chair, listening for sounds that rarely come, rather than running from something.

If something scary does happen, it will likely not be nearly as momentous as what television has made us believe. We are told ghosts are scary. I would amend that to say, in most cases, ghosts are startling and creepy, and we are expecting to be terrified in the dark. I have most definitely freaked myself out at a haunted location, or been nervous to walk down a dark hallway, I assure you, but I never once feared for my life in a real way. There are stories from friends, more seasoned investigators, who have seen some deep Dark stuff, but I haven't encountered anything even close to a demon or malicious spirit. In reality, when I've brought first-timers along with me, more than once, they've turned to me at the end of the night and said, "That wasn't as scary as I thought it would be." My first time out at Fort Mifflin was unique; in all my investigations since that first time, maybe only once or twice have I gotten that level of activity. Some nights are scary and special, and some are... well... boring. Maybe I'm tempting Fate. Maybe one day, I'll eat these words and need to publish a retraction, but it would have to be a pretty intense experience indeed. If we go into locations expecting demonic activity, we can easily lose focus on the research while we are there and close ourselves off to any activity at all.

Another frequent question is along the lines of "Aren't you afraid something will follow you home?" The answer? Sometimes, but not enough to stop me. When I began, the idea of something clinging to me after I'd left a location, also known as an attachment, really made me uncomfortable. I'd heard some scary tales from investigators about spirits that stayed with them after an investigation, for varying lengths of time and varying levels of disturbances in their lives, and I questioned how responsible I was being, considering I have two young children at home. A lot of investigators and witchcraft-practicing friends encourage some type of personal protection when engaging with the paranormal – carrying various crystals or a rosary, for example. Some say to leave your shoes outside upon returning home from a haunted place. Burning sage or palo santo to cleanse your space is a fairly common home-cleansing ritual across many belief systems. As a pleasantly scented candle might soothe anxiety, the ritualistic burning of sage might bring comfort to another. Is this a self-fulfilling act of sorts? Maybe.

On the flipside, I've had conversations with investigators who warn against too much personal protection – in theory, we are going into these places to speak with spirits, and if we are actively protecting ourselves from their getting comfortable with us enough to connect, aren't we shooting ourselves in the foot? In the end, it comes down to what habits and practices help you feel grounded and safe, but still open enough to interact with "Other."

Personally, on investigation days, I spend time with family in the hours leading up to my heading out the door, and wear jewelry gifted to me with love during the investigation. When I return home, I shower as soon as it is feasible (sometimes the next morning if my family is sleeping soundly when I arrive home at 4 a.m.) and cuddle my dog for some peace. Only once or twice have I felt the presence of a lingering spirit once I returned home, and one of these times I think it was more that I was still feeling a little leftover fear and adrenaline from my night's adventures. In both cases, the sensations dissipated within a day, and I never felt like I was in danger.

An additional side note regarding the fear factor in investigating is that, although rare, we must always remember to be vigilant for intentional fear cues. Some "haunted" locations will tell outright fabrications about the history of their "dark entities" to enhance the appeal of their location in this ever-growing (and ever-profitable) field. Some might purposefully not restore a decaying area for that chic creepy aesthetic, or put in deliberately uneven flooring so your body is physically unstable and thus prompted for anxiety.

Though very rare indeed, some location owners go even further with piped-in infrasound to throw you off your guard. Infrasound is a low-frequency sound wave, generally 20 Hz, which is widely believed to be below the limit of human audibility. Reported effects of long exposure to infrasound include uncomfortable sensations in your heart, feelings of vertigo, nausea, and imbalance, all of which can contribute to a general sense of fearful discomfort. Sometimes a constant low sound from an appliance or other piece of electronic equipment can cause this effect naturally. It is sometimes used sparingly in horror movie soundtracks to add extra tension. In an interesting paper published in 1998, Vic Tandy and Dr. Tony Lawrence of Coventry University wrote a paper called "Ghosts in the Machine" for the *Journal of the Society for Psychical Research*, describing their research suggesting that an infrasonic signal of 19 Hz might be responsible for some ghost sightings and paranormal claims.[3]

If we hope to progress as a field to be taken more seriously, the act of faking or intentionally misleading investigators must be called out and ended. Creating false positives for investigators who fall prey to the deceit creates even more chaos in a field that already gets its fair share of dubious side-eye. Furthermore, if a location is indeed haunted, this behavior is even more distracting and despicable. Spirits should be allowed to interact for themselves, if they desire to, without the hindrances of false cues getting in the way. This type of intentional fearmongering is disrespectful to both the living and dead alike.

Once you've done your homework and feel you are investigating a location with trustworthy caretakers, with the real history in hand and a mostly level head on your shoulders, the next step is to stay open to what weirdness may be in store. This part is easier said than done. An open mind and an open heart are integral to connecting with spirit. Your bodily senses will be your best indicators of what is really happening around you, not the beep of a flashy piece of tech or another person in the group telling you what you are feeling. If you are lucky and patient, you might get that gut feeling that you are in the midst of witnessing something paranormal. You must go in with the confidence that no one has any more sway over spirit activity than anyone else; we all have a part to play and a right to study it.

This is the kind of hobby that either grips you from the beginning, or it doesn't. If you find something drawing you into research of the dead, follow the thread. Though I haven't been "doing this for twenty years as a clairvoyant psychic," I have experienced enough strange activity to change some of my original beliefs on the paranormal. I like to think I'm reasonable and educated enough to know when I'm witnessing something explainable by logic, and when I've seen something truly odd. I am by no means attempting to convert any skeptics into paranormal believers; I simply have a few stories to tell, from the perspective of an average mom who happens to prioritize spooky stuff. What follows is a glimpse into my spooky adventures so far, and what I've learned about hauntings, the paranormal community, and myself along the way.

PART TWO

INVESTIGATING THE
PARANORMAL

CHAPTER II
SECRET SPOOKY
ROOMMATE

L ong before I became a paranormal investigator, before marriage or children, I was your average college student, living in a ratty apartment with five of my friends. I attended a large university in Pennsylvania, a decision made mostly because I wanted to have the same alma mater as my older brother. I didn't always love going home for the summer, so when spring semester ended, I often stayed on campus and took summer classes, or just enjoyed the quiet freedom of my college town in the off-season.

During summer break before my junior year, my brother and sister-in-law came to visit and stayed at my apartment while my other roommates were gone. They bunked in the room I shared with my friend during the school year, and I borrowed another roommate's room across the hall for the night. We had gone out for a few drinks, as you do when you're in college and trying to look cool in front of your big brother, though we only had a few. (My sister-in-law was pregnant at the time, and we didn't want her to feel too left out while she abstained.) We headed back to my apartment, watched a movie, and went to bed.

Sometime later, I suddenly woke up out of a dead sleep because my nose was freezing cold. I reached up to cover my cold nose with my hand, drowsily coming around to full consciousness, when I realized I could see my breath in front of me in the muted glow from the streetlamp filtering in through the blinds. The room was absolutely freezing. Even in my sleep-addled mind I knew this was unusual – it was summer, and though my apartment building was a little shabby, I'd never recalled it being drafty or found the heating system to be unreliable. Our apartment building had originally been one big house, then renovated into twelve apartments, four on each of three floors, and was not luxurious enough to boast a powerful air-conditioning unit; constant box fans were necessities of every roommate, myself included. However, even though I momentarily noted the strangeness of the cold, I didn't think too much about it; sometimes nights in Pennsylvania did get a little chilly. I brushed it off as a weird weather anomaly and set my sights on finding a hoodie to cozy into and getting right back to sleep.

I sat up fully, about to pillage my friend's closet, when across the room, about three feet away, her computer turned on, the bluish glow softly illuminating the desk and chair as it booted up. It was in that moment I suddenly felt the creepy feeling that I now search for as a paranormal investigator all these years later: that something unseen was in the room with me, and I was not alone. I sat stock-still as my pulse picked up, watching as the computer went through its various normal start-up processes. After a few moments (thankfully without Captain Howdy from *The Exorcist* mysteriously appearing on the screen), I bolstered the courage to slowly get up and turn off the computer. I waited a few moments to see if it would turn on again, then checked the power strip it was plugged into, but nothing looked amiss. I still had that eerie feeling swirling around me, and I desperately wanted to go wake my brother. But as I moved to the bedroom door and opened it, the room suddenly felt normal again, as if some spell had been broken. I hesitated in the hallway, hand raised to knock, but in the end, I didn't want to interrupt their sleep for no real reason now that the odd moment had passed. I crept back into the bedroom, crawled back into my friend's bed, and was able to sleep until morning.

When I mentioned it at breakfast, my family hadn't been awakened or noticed anything odd in the night, and my roommates had never had an unexplainable experience in that room. Was this another moment in my timeline when the paranormal was "checking in" on me? What would have happened next if I hadn't tried to leave the room? Maybe that had been a moment in which I could have begun my paranormal journey, but something in me unconsciously said, "Wait."

CHAPTER 12
FIRST THINGS FIRST

In relating how my macabre adventures shook up my life and rejuvenated my dull "stuck in mom mode" feeling, there will inevitably be some moments of confusion. Try as I might to keep things palatably "normal" for those readers outside the paranormal community, it's difficult, no, scratch that – it's impossible – to relay firsthand paranormal stories without addressing some of the theories and common terminology in the field, as wild as some of them sound at first. If you can broaden your mind and reach into the Weird with me, I'll explain concepts as I go, to accomplish at least a basic understanding of some ideas that paranormal investigators use to guide our actions and interpret evidence. And I speak from experience when I say you just never know what idea might really resonate with you and pull you down the rabbit hole of further independent research.

Before diving into any accounts from my actual investigations, two widely held paranormal points must be tackled first, and you may not like them:

1. "Orbs" in photographs are not ghosts.
2. Phantom faces in photos are usually a result of something called *pareidolia*.

Here comes the hate mail. Sometimes in the paranormal field, and even to those with a casual interest as well, doubting the validity of orbs and faces captured in photographs will be a point of serious contention. People often feel very strongly about their evidence and experiences and will vehemently defend them. To be taken seriously, however, truth must be the priority, and if a photo can be disproven, it must be set aside. Most "orbs" are dust particles, insects, droplets of water, or other naturally occurring particulates in the environment catching light, or even reflections from light sources. I've nearly been duped by rod-shaped anomalies in photos that I later realized resulted from slow shutter speed in a dark environment. There *are* accounts of light-emanating anomalies at haunted locations, and nothing in the paranormal can be a 100% blanket statement. However, this one may as well be, considering the number of unimpressive orb photos circulating in this community.

I have very little bandwidth for considering faces captured in photographs (and a generally poor poker face to go with it, to the occasional dismay of said enthusiastic photo-holders.) Like orbs, these perceived anomalies are often the result of something called "pareidolia." Pareidolia is the tendency of our brains to try to make sense of random visual patterns by perceiving them as a specific, identifiable image.[4] Our brains prefer something they can understand. Common examples include seeing shapes in clouds, faces in rocks, or ghostly visages in a reflection on a windowpane. The closely related term "apophenia" is also sometimes used, though that technically is in reference to meaningful patterns perceived in random or unrelated information and ideas versus *visual* patterns.[5] I always jokingly compare apophenia to my (slightly pathetic) schoolgirl crushes, where a single glance from the cute boy paired with his later request to borrow a pencil was perceived by me as an undeniable return of my affection. In this self-deprecating example, my strong wish for confirmation of his mutual crush fueled my conclusion, when eventually I had to come to the sad realization that the poor guy just needed a pencil that day, and I was sitting nearest to him. Apophenia: the bane of boy-crazy teenage girls everywhere.

It can be tricky to tactfully debunk, or ideally sidestep altogether, "ghost" photos that individuals are excited to share. In general, people do not like their evidence to be disputed. I understand; it's easy to get whipped up into a frenzy of excitement when you believe you've caught something unusual. When cold reality knocks you down a peg, a normal human reaction can often be defensiveness and sometimes even bristly anger. As such, I like to avoid seeing casual investigators' "ghost photos" altogether, if I can help it.

These hard truths are lessons you hopefully learn early in the field, like I did, bumbling my way through footage, wanting desperately to see evidence of a spirit but having more experienced investigators dismiss a lot of what I presented without batting an eye. You develop a better knack for debunking, and gain confidence with experience, as in any field. You learn to toss questionable photos to the side, resulting in stronger, more exciting evidence when something really does make the cut. In my experience, truly compelling, shareable evidence is hard to come by, but every time I search for it, it's a thrill.

CHAPTER 13
SELMA MANSION
NORRISTOWN, PENNSYLVANIA

A few enthusiastic months into my boots-on-the-ground paranormal journey, I was invited by a friend I'd met at Fort Mifflin to investigate Selma Mansion in Norristown, Pennsylvania, less than twenty minutes from my home. I was excited to explore a haunted house and be able to fall asleep in my own bed at the end of the night. I didn't realize at the time that I was stepping into a haunted location that would become such a big part of my paranormal journey, almost like a classroom of sorts as I got acquainted with different paranormal techniques and theories.

Selma Mansion has been home to many prominent families in Pennsylvania's history through the years, many of whom had a significant impact on the development of the community and the current size and importance of the city of Norristown as it is today. Originally, the mansion was built in 1794 as home to General Andrew Porter and his family. Andrew Porter was a Marine captain in the Revolutionary War and later a brigadier general in the Pennsylvania militia. He was also, notably, the great-grandfather of Mary Todd Lincoln, who would become the wife of President Abraham Lincoln.

Andrew Porter's sons went on to successful and impactful careers in the public eye, as governors, military leaders, and even the Secretary of War under President Tyler. In 1821, after the death of General Porter and his widow, Selma Mansion became the property of the Andrew Knox family. Knox was a former shipping merchant from Savannah, Georgia, who in 1853 divided some of the estate land into lots, beginning the development of that section of the current city of Norristown. After Knox passed away, the residence and remaining property went to his daughter Ellen and her husband, Joseph Fornance, who was a prominent lawyer and president of the Historical Society of Montgomery County. After their deaths in the late 1920s, Selma Mansion passed to the ownership of their son, Major Joseph Knox Fornance, and his wife, Ruth. After Ruth passed away in 1983, the house remained largely unoccupied until the Norristown Preservation Society stepped in to restore what they could.[6] It wasn't long before those volunteering in the mansion's upkeep began to notice that perhaps the house was not, in fact, as unoccupied as they previously thought. Disembodied voices, sudden temperature fluctuations, and indications of a seemingly angry spirit in the basement (who prefers to be called "sir") soon became standard experiences on the property. The Preservation Society embraced their active unseen guests and began offering overnight paranormal investigations to interested parties.

That first night in October 2020, I arrived with my then-teammate, and on our way in, we were introduced to two women who have since become friends. There were only five of us investigating, and I was relieved and excited that we were a small group and had the entire building to ourselves. As we settled in the "safe room," loading bags onto the empty tables and signing liability waivers, the mansion board member who served as the paranormal liaison informed us to "never go to the third floor alone."

After that ominous declaration, our host left for the night, and we began. We headed up to the second level for our initial sweep, to get a feel for the place and check standard EMF levels, and we each instantly sensed some kind of eerie energy there. As we began the investigation proper, we were just settling onto some couches in a second-floor drawing room after setting up some equipment. Like the flip of a switch, I suddenly felt intense frustration with every person in the room. I had instantly liked the other women I had just met, and I obviously liked my other two friends and had no reason to be irritated with them. I was holding a video camera, leaning against an old sofa, and I remember asking myself, "Why do I want to scream at these people?" They were just chatting amiably before we got truly settled into the quiet, and I was livid. My friend moved slightly on the floor, making the wood creak quietly under his foot, and I had to stop myself from rolling my eyes or releasing an impatient huff. I felt these aggravations but said nothing – I barely knew two of the people there and didn't want their first impression of me to include my saying how much I disliked them all in that moment. The sentiments angrily roiling around my mind were completely foreign to both my mood and my opinion of the people there; I knew something unusual was happening, though I had never experienced anything like it before.

BORROWED EMOTIONS, STONE TAPE THEORY, AND RESIDUAL VS INTELLIGENT HAUNTINGS

This sensation of experiencing emotions that are not your own is part of a paranormal theory in which lingering spiritual emotional energy in a space can affect you. This rabbit hole topic may sound familiar in theory, if not by name – Stone Tape theory.

Stone Tape theory is the speculation that ghosts are like a recording, able to be played back via the nearby environment under the right conditions.[7,8,9] It is the idea that mental impressions of strong emotional or traumatic events can be projected outward in the form of energy, recorded or "taped" onto rock/stones (especially limestone and quartz), physical elements of a location, or even items in a home, and replayed now and again. The energy may manifest as apparitions, visions, or as strong emotional responses, like what I experienced at Selma Mansion. The idea has its roots in the work of such early psychic researchers as Charles Babbage and Eleonor Sidgwick. It's an extension of the concept of a room "feeling heavy" after an argument – almost as if someone walking in after a fight can sense that it happened. The Stone Tape theory can be said to also be in play when an antique or oddities shop claims they have a haunted item for sale. The item, in theory, is holding either a spirit or the impression of a powerful moment from its history.

Stone Tape theory loops in the common belief in residual spirits – entities who do not have conscious thought and who are sort of like shimmers of previous souls "going through the motions," so to speak. This is in tandem to intelligent spirits, entities who are well aware that you are speaking to them, and may even respond with meaningful answers to your inquiries in whatever way they are able.

I personally have, in my opinion, come across the exact phenomena of both Stone Tape theory and a residual haunting at least twice in my adventures (probably more), Selma Mansion being one of them. The "borrowed emotion" I felt in that room was most definitely not of internal origin. I believe I was feeling an emotion of a past argument or period of turmoil from previous residents in that house, the energy of which I caught in a psychic way.

After a while, we decided to move on, to my relief. Upon leaving that room, I felt much calmer and held none of the animosity I had been feeling minutes before. I believe I had been experiencing secondhand emotion, either from a nearby spirit or leftover energy in the space. This, of course, is the type of evidence that isn't truly compelling unless you are the one experiencing it. I have no evidence to show how I was feeling, let alone why.

∼

That evening, a little while later, we set up some proximity sensors behind us on the stairs as we climbed to the third floor, one on the staircase directly off the floor below, and one on the landing between floors. After spending some time in the nursery and adjacent room without much activity, we crossed the darkened hall. As the last of us passed through the threshold, everyone's attention on how creepy the decrepit bathroom ahead looked in the dark, the first sensor went off. The wail of the sudden alarm rang sharply in my ears, startling my heart up into my throat. I remember the chills I had in that moment. I gasped with shock and instantly began rolling video on my phone camera. A moment later, the closer sensor, a music box, activated, its eerie blue light and creepy melody filling the stairwell. I couldn't believe both sensors had gone off, as if someone were climbing the stairs, coming towards us.

Paranormal television would have you believe these sensors go off dozens of times throughout the night at each investigation; in reality, that is rarely the case. To have two different sensors go off and even indicate direction of movement is an incredible circumstance.

I stood stock-still a step back from the top of the stairwell, eyes glued to the blue glow from the music box. I hoped to glimpse a shadow on the landing or any kind of movement coming towards me, but there was nothing more. We invited the unseen presence to join us in the room we entered, but all was quiet, for the moment.

ELECTRONIC VOICE PHENOMENA

Instrumental transcommunication, often abbreviated to ITC, refers to all forms of spirit communication using any kind of electronic device. An electronic voice phenomenon, or EVP, one of the most striking pieces of ITC evidence that can be captured, is a voice or human noise that is audible on a recording, but not heard at the time. There are, of course, audible phenomena, including disembodied voices and sounds we hear without the aid of recording technology, such as the voice we heard in casemate 5 at Fort Mifflin.

If collected properly, carefully avoiding contamination from background noise, whispering, or voices of those investigators present, an EVP can give truly meaningful clues as to the ghostly manifestations on a property. EVPs do not pull from local radio signals or prerecorded word or voice banks like some of the tech we see used on paranormal television; they are simply recording the audio around us.

As a note, in an EVP session, it is considered good practice to "tag" any sound you notice that is definitively not paranormal, such as a sniffle, a rumbling stomach, a whisper from a team member, or a car going by. For example, if I move my foot and a floorboard creaks, I will say, "That's my foot." Doing so helps investigators discount odd noises when reviewing evidence later, which they might otherwise have mistaken as ghostly.

There are some common classifications of EVP recordings that investigators use to differentiate the quality and relative impressiveness of a capture. Each is defined by a rather subjective set of parameters, as seen below:[10]

Class A – This type of EVP is loud, easily understandable by multiple individuals, and very clear, so much so that it does not need enhancement or amplification to be understood.

Class B – This is the most common class of EVP; it is of somewhat lesser clarity but is still audible with only minor enhancement. The voice may not be clear enough to be totally understood, and there may be disagreement as to what is being said.

Class C – This is the lowest-quality EVP; there may even be doubt as to whether or not an EVP is actually present on the recording.

Class D – Most investigators do not even acknowledge Class D EVPs, but instead consider them as "possible" moments of interest for further review. Class D EVPs are not words, they are usually sounds: whispers, breathing noises, etc.

L ater in the evening, we filed into the kitchen and planted ourselves around the small table there. We began an EVP session, asking various questions to the stillness around us. At one otherwise silent moment, we all heard a male voice gruffly mumble something from the direction of the third floor. We had just come from there and thus knew it was empty. We asked a few more questions, hoping to engage the same activity, but it was seemingly quiet, and we decided to chalk the brief voice up to possible outside contamination, though we didn't see anyone on the property. Sometimes, in these quiet moments on an investigation, normal conversations amongst team members inevitably begin – six hours investigating in complete silence is unlikely, whoever you are. Sometimes in these moments, when we are not so wholly focused on the spirits, is when they communicate most often.

Our group was still in the kitchen, and having not heard anything unusual for a few minutes, we started chatting about what life must have been like in the 1800s. A few of our group were ruminating on family structure in the days of the mansion at its prime: did the entire family live here? Who cared for the elderly in their later years? We hadn't heard anything more, and we eventually moved on from the room.

After an investigation, I review every second of footage I filmed, for both visual and audio anomalies. During this conversation in the kitchen, unbeknownst to us, we caught one of the most stunning EVPs I've ever heard.

As my friend finishes a sentence, and just as another friend begins to respond, a separate female voice says three syllables. It's quite clearly none of us, and the voice comes from a position in the room with us. To my ears, after hundreds of listens, I believe the voice is saying "What are you?" It seems a strange question for as spirit to ask, but upon contemplation, and based on experiences after that night, I think there is a reason behind it. One of the women we met that night, and one of the two women in the conversation at the time of the EVP, is a self-proclaimed psychic medium. While I do not put much stake in the ever-growing crowd of individuals who claim to have psychic ability, I have worked alongside this particular friend since that first night and believe in her abilities. Regardless, in other investigations since we met at Selma, I have heard other audio devices refer to her "beautiful light" and similarly refer-encing that she "looks different" than the other investigators present. I have thought whether the EVP asking "What are you?" is referring to her and wondering to themselves why she looks different. If my friend indeed hears spirits and interacts differently with spirit energy than I do, maybe she physically looks different to them. Maybe she looks brighter or clearer through the Veil compared to the rest of us. It's an interesting idea.

When we concluded our EVP session without getting any activity, or so we thought at the time, we decided to move to the front parlor and try our hand at a different method to attempt spirit contact, the Estes Method.

THE ESTES METHOD

The Estes Method is an experimental technique to attempt verbal communication with spirits. It was conceived in 2016 by paranormal researchers Karl Pfeiffer, Connor Randall, and Michelle Tate and has been gaining steady popularity in the community, especially after being featured on a few recent paranormal television shows and documentaries. It's exciting and can yield fascinating results, and it's fairly accessible – requiring very little in the way of tech or expertise. It does, however, require at least two partners with a high level of trust and a desire for honest results.

One of the partners, the "listener or receiver," sits with noise-canceling headphones and a blindfold, listening only to static white noise or, more commonly, a Spirit Box.

The Spirit Box, often model name "SB-7" and referred to as such, is a device that rapidly scans through radio stations, either forward or backward. (A quick note: while there is a "reverse" option on the device, this does not play the voice clips backward; it merely reverses the station scanning order.) The receiver is listening for a multisyllabic word or phrase from either the SB-7 or through the static noise, which he or she simply repeats out loud without being able to hear their partner. It's critical to get familiar with the rhythm of the device and not jump onto every half-word with too much enthusiasm. The listener may also experience visual stimuli, physical sensations, or intense feelings while they are "under," which they should also relay verbally to their partner.

Their partner, who cannot hear the SB-7 or the static, meanwhile asks questions of the spirit. Ideally, meaningful and properly timed responses stated by the receiver will sync up and indicate direct responses.

The concept behind the method is to remove the inevitable human bias toward hearing an answer to a question asked. If the person deciphering the voices heard on the device doesn't know what questions are being asked, and the answer makes sense (i.e., partner asks: "How many people are in this room?" and the listener answers: "Three"), the evidence is more compelling that a spirit is engaging in conversation. If the listener repeats what he or she hears, and what is said is a reasonable, corresponding answer to a question, we can use the dialogue to lead a conversation with spirits for more in-depth communication. [11]

It is also thought that this method of mild sensory deprivation provides a distraction to let the active mind wander and more fully tune into images and thoughts seen by one's third eye. Some investigators take even further steps with full sensory deprivation or red light shining into the receiver's closed eyes, hypnosis, or meditation during a session. Some variations place the listener alone in a room while the partner uses a phone to relay whispered questions from another room entirely. Some groups run multiple simultaneous Estes sessions, with two or more listeners at the same time. The method is all based on conjecture and pseudoscience, of course, but it's been an interesting facet to add to my investigations through the years.

On this particular night at Selma Mansion in 2020, our group used a white noise generator, headphones, and a blindfold to diminish outside influences as we strained to listen and understand voices from the unknown. Our session resulted in very little to go on, and it was the last technique we employed before leaving for the night. I have found time and again that the conclusion of our investigations at Selma seem to be deemed by the spirits themselves; each time it is as though the spirits are as ready for us to leave as we are to go, and they quiet down for the evening, urging our departure.

I n the years since my first visit there, I have returned several times to Selma Mansion during daytime events to support the various fundraisers they hold. The building is an integral part of the region's paranormal community, and a lot of teams consider Selma to be their paranormal "home base," so to speak. There are a lot of social functions on the property, with a lot of the same friendly faces in the crowd time and again. I've even brought my children, who instantly requested to race up to the third floor after I told them about the old "creepy dolls" and antique toys in what was once the nursery. There was a moment when they looked together out one of the windows in an upstairs room to take in the sunny view outside, and I laughed to myself – I was now so far deep into the paranormal that it was nothing to me to bring my children to the house where I had captured a startling EVP not so long before.

I was very eager to return to Selma Mansion for an investigation, but it was nearly eighteen months after that first overnight experience that I was able to do so. I hoped to directly contact the same spirits with whom I had interacted on my last investigation. Perhaps by now they might recognize me from my many visits and be more open to engaging with me.

The property caretaker we had met that first night (and whose name is changed here for his family's privacy) had become a friendly acquaintance over the months since that first night, and he had been helpful in keeping me informed of goings-on at Selma Mansion. He reached out with fundraiser invitations and news, and we had occasional conversations about mutual friends or paranormal experiences. Unfortunately, last winter he got very sick, and his illness took him from this world within mere months. It was an odd feeling; though I'd worked with him arranging the details of my group's next overnight investigation, by the time the scheduled date arrived, he was no longer Earthside to greet me there. To many, he embodied Selma's paranormal reputation, he was its champion, and it had always been clear that the property and its spirits were very dear to him.

JUNE 2022

As I made my way to the mansion, I felt sure that I wouldn't call on my friend in the investigation ahead; it felt wrong to use a recent passing as a trigger of sorts. He hadn't been a close friend, and his family was still very much grieving, so while I planned to privately whisper a greeting, I hadn't intended on calling out to him for an equipment response or anything filmed. My goal was to go back to revisit previous experiences and see if similar phenomena occurred, or if I could debunk a little better, having much more experience investigating than my initial overnight on the property. My investigating partners were meeting me there: my best friend of twenty plus years, and a friend I'd met through social media, whom I was excited to meet. She had much more experience than myself, and as our group was so small, I was going to take the opportunity to pick her brain.

Luckily, our online friendship instantly sprang into real camaraderie. We began our investigation in the basement, trying to contact the spirit I've been told prefers to be called "sir." In all my visits, I'd never been down to the basement. It was classically creepy, a nightmare basement if there ever was one.

We had two interesting experiences in that dusty basement, both of which were debunked eventually, but in the moment were quite spooky. An EVP session proved to be fruitless, as just outside the basement point of egress, the summer evening was warm and lovely, and the neighbors were outside enjoying themselves – loudly. So instead, we sat in the provided folding chairs in one half of the bisected basement, listening for any sign of movement within the room. We had proximity detectors set up in the middle area, where the stairwell up to the kitchen was located. After a few moments, in which we had lapsed into conversation, we all noticed a flash of light on the opposite side of the basement. We had a few frightening moments where it appeared to be a glimmering human shape steadily approaching us, but after a lengthy pause, we determined that a faint light filtering through weeds in the ceiling-level window were playing optical tricks on our eyes. I just hope I didn't bruise my new friend's arm too badly with my intensifying grip as the "shimmering man" came toward us.

The second experience in the basement was rather odd and

vaguely disgusting – a strong onion scent that seemed to come and go and made us all comically smell ourselves and confirm that we had each applied deodorant that day. The pungent odor would hit intensely and then fade a moment later, at which point I would sometimes feel something looming at my back, about to reach out and touch me. It never did, though, and I was forced to consider that I was letting my mind run away with my rationality. Though in the moment I thought it was odd that it would come and go even though we were sitting still, the basement floor was uneven, dirt patches in some corners, and there was moisture in the air. It made sense that odd smells may waft through on small breezes through the small but visible cracks in the walls. Upon further research, I later found that some molds smell strongly of onion, not to mention, of course, that wild spring onions are common in the area, and we were, indeed, partially underground.

The most compelling part of the evening occurred at the tail end of the night, an hour or so past when we considered wrapping up, but decided to eke out just a bit more time. A last-minute decision to stay a little longer and investigate upstairs had us setting up the EMF tripwire (a six-foot-long strand of lights, each independently acting as a K2 meter, changing colors to indicate a nearby change in the magnetic field) by the door. My friend set up her REM-Pod and music box in the adjacent hallway, out of our line of sight, but close enough that we would hear it from the next room. I perched my video camera recording the devices, fingers crossed. We settled into the room in which I'd experienced the sudden angry feelings a few years prior, and ran a short-burst EVP session, in which we review for responses immediately after wrapping up the session. This is a great way to continue meaningful communication with a spirit, as ideally we can ask follow-up questions to any responses we might receive. It was late into the evening, and the neighborhood had presumably gone to bed for the night. The session was quiet, a quick review yielding no responses, so we decided to add in the Spirit Box. I turned it on and placed it on a nearby chair for us all to listen and decipher together any messages that might come through.

The lights on the tripwire by the doorway remained a steadfast purple; the Spirit Box continued its scrolling shushes and word fragments. After a few moments, a scratchy, accented male voice started to periodically come through. We acknowledged the voice and started asking more questions, and as sentence fragments came through bit by bit, the responses painted for us a picture of a young man who possibly used to work as a custodian on the property.

"I work here... cleaning..." and similar responses came through more and more clearly.

The voice grew easier to understand as the strings of words became longer. Wanting to hone in on a possible time period of this spirit a bit more, I ran down my mental list of known previous occupants in the house, hoping to trigger more on the Spirit Box or the tripwire, which had remained steadfastly purple.

I asked with long pauses in between, "Do you know Mary?... Mr. Fornance?... Mr. Knox?"

Nothing.

I can't say what made me break my own previous decision not to call on my recently deceased friend at this moment, maybe I was just getting tired, and I didn't think I'd get any more of a response than with the other names that hadn't stirred anything. But I suddenly heard myself asking, with a little hesitation before I spoke, "Do you know Tim?"

Fireworks. Each individual light on the tripwire lit up like the Fourth of July, and I gasped in shock. The timing was impeccable – and the energy in the room shifted on a dime.

The tripwire had been totally still the entire session, and at this personal, emotional question, it went wild. A heartbeat later, my friend repeated my question, and the scratchy male voice came through again on the Spirit Box: "I know Tim."

I was floored. It was the type of experience that hits you in your gut if you are there in the room. It was compelling not only because of the timing of the equipment activity together, but with that visceral feeling of "Other" that was suddenly there in the room, which cannot be captured by video or audio recordings. Something tells me it wasn't Tim himself, but with his having spent so much time on-site, I am completely unsurprised that the spirits in the house knew him and were pleased I did too. It's likely they mourn his loss as the living do.

A few minutes later, I attempted to confirm their presence again on the lights, specifically asking for them to touch the tripwire, and they did. As minutes passed, we started to notice the voice started to come through haltingly and not as consistently, as if it was getting tired, its energy reserves too low after having dazzled us. We felt the energy quieting, floating away on an intangible breeze. The room and the house seemed to grow sleepy, ready to shut down for the evening. We took the hint, thanked the spirits, and wrapped up our night.

Sometimes I feel pangs of jealousy watching friends visit larger haunted sites, with legendary ghostly claims and sprawling grounds. While I check a few epic spots off my bucket list here and there at a leisurely pace, I often wish I could visit a slew of them rapid-fire, to keep up with the spooky Joneses. However, in practicing active gratitude, I am cognizant of how lucky I am to be able to investigate the same haunted spaces multiple times. In doing so, not only do you become more familiar with the flow of the building and its normal noises, but perhaps, like Selma Mansion, the resident spirits get to know you, too.

CHAPTER 14
ELKS LODGE
TAMAQUA, PENNSYLVANIA

O n the main street in the small town of Tamaqua, Pennsylvania, sits the Elks Club building, home to the local Benevolent and Protective Order of Elks, a co-ed fraternal organization originally founded in 1868. This particular building holds a bowling alley in the basement, a bar on the ground floor, meeting rooms above, and finally, unoccupied, decaying apartments adjacent to a grand ball-room on top. What an amalgamation of spaces piled on top of one another. I have been to the Elks Club twice, once during the day and once at night, to look into its claims, which range from footsteps to disembodied voices, to sightings and claims of a negative entity inhabiting the upstairs apartments. My teammate at the time and I were invited to the premises by a mutual friend, and I personally was quite excited to investigate the claims of a haunted bowling alley in particular, simply for the uniqueness of the setting.

Unfortunately, on my first visit, though sitting in the middle of a bowling alley lane in the dark was an undoubtedly unique spot to investigate, I did not feel any presence of "Other," nor did I gather any kind of ghostly evidence of note on that floor. The apartment level above, however, was another story.

As you reach the very top level of the Tamaqua Elks building, you can feel that the energy is different, as though when you step off the last stair, you are stepping through some kind of heavy, invisible veil. Turning left and walking the creaky wooden hallway toward the two apartments at the very end, that ominous feeling in your stomach grows, the one that tells you to turn around, go back downstairs, go play pool or bowl a few frames instead of continuing on your path. But on an investigation night, that's the feeling you follow, against your instincts for safety, like swimming opposite the current in a river.

The hallway shows evidence of past Halloween parties – purposeful red-paint-splattered handprints dragged along the yellowed wall, old props slumped against doorframes of bathrooms in varying states of decay. An old, dusty upright piano sits unused in the hallway – it calls out to you to play a sad, lonely key as you squeeze by. However, it is the last two apartment doors at the far end, side by side, where I feel most uncomfortable.

The term "apartment" here is used generously, I might add – each apartment is the size of a modest bedroom, if that. The room on the left was, at the time of my visits, crowded with discarded medical equipment, crutches, and packs of adult diapers. There were filing cabinets packed with old patient records next to overturned furniture and swaths of ripped wallpaper curls. By contrast, the apartment on the right is completely bare save an old drum covered in a tarp on the far wall, and a folding chair.

The first strange experience I encountered in this area was just as I crossed over the threshold to the cluttered apartment. I was feeling the buzz of energy surrounding these rooms as I approached, and when I stepped over the doorway to get a better peek inside, I suddenly tasted an extremely bitter taste on my tongue. I was startled – I had recently had a sip of soda on a break between sessions; there was no reason a lingering food flavor should suddenly be noticeable, especially such an unpleasant one. Later research for explanations for a sudden bad taste on the tongue has not proven helpful in debunking – I'd like to declare that I brush and floss regularly, thank you very much. I was also not pregnant at the time; sudden bitterness in the mouth can sometimes occur in pregnant women. Nor did I have acid reflux, a vitamin overdose, recent head trauma, or effects from any medication, as I had taken none. [12] I'm left to ponder if this was indeed my first experience with "clairgustience," a type of intuitive ability in which one can "taste" paranormal phenomena.

INTUITIVE ABILITIES

One unusual concept I think a lot of paranormal newcomers don't know from the get-go is that individuals receive paranormal information in different ways. Some have a natural inclination for one way over another, and some individuals, presumably including many a skeptic, seem to have none at all – at least that they will admit. Most researchers would agree that there are six different types of "clair" senses (from the French for "clear"), which may or may not work in tandem with one another. Each "clair" ability more or less matches our basic human senses. In a brief overview, they are:

Clairvoyance ("clear sight") – An individual can interpret a paranormal experience in a visual way; they see spirit in the form of an apparition, shadow figure, light anomaly, or shimmer in the air.

Clairaudience ("clear sound") – An individual interprets the paranormal in an auditory way. They may hear a disembodied voice, cough, laugh, or growl. They may also hear a spirit speaking directly to them.

Clairsentience ("clear feeling") – An individual may interpret the paranormal literally via physical touch, but in a deeper meaning, this refers more to picking up psychically on emotion or the *feeling* of spirit nearby. I usually refer to clairsentience as it pertains to that "gut feeling" of feeling something in the vicinity.

Claircognizance ("clear knowing") – This is much related to clairsentience in that it is a gut feeling, but more of a gut *knowing*. An individual may just know facts about the history, location, or nearby spirit without knowing how they know it.

Clairalience/Clairsalience ("clear scent") – The final two intuitive abilities on this list are perhaps the weirdest, all things considered. Clairalience is when paranormal phenomena are picked up through scent. An individual may smell unexplained perfume, flowers, tobacco, or more grimly, decay or rot. A note: "phantom smells" can often be explained naturally – through porous surfaces nearby. For example, wood beams in an old home will hold the odor of cigar smoke for a surprising amount of time. On a wet day, as moisture hits the porous surface, scent particles will be released easily, so use caution in declaring this ability, only after due diligence.

Clairgustience ("clear taste") – The winner of "Weirdest Intuitive Ability," in my humble opinion, is when an individual perceives paranormal phenomena via taste. Individuals reporting this ability claim to taste various foods, blood, and even "fear," however that might taste, when encountering the paranormal.[13]

Some intuitive abilities appear to bloom and strengthen over time. There is a belief that these senses may be trained to grow stronger, either intentionally with study or just with repeated exposure to the right conditions. Additionally, the concept of psychometry, in which an individual holds or touches a paranormally active item or part of the environment, is thought to sharpen innate psychic abilities through direct physical contact.

I doubted the existence of clairgustience altogether until it happened to me, when I suddenly tasted the bitterness of medication on my tongue when I entered that room. I haven't experienced clairgustience since that time, which makes me wonder if you can have flashes of these abilities without retaining them permanently. Perhaps my doubt in the ability is what hinders it from developing further. My skeptical side can't help but suggest that I had an undetectable and unpleasant burp or something easily explainable at the moment. The paranormal is frustratingly indeterminate sometimes, dotted with a lot of individuals seeking attention for their "gifts," real or not.

On my second investigation at the Elks Lodge, in the evening versus my daytime trip, we again spent time in the less-cluttered abandoned apartment at the end of the hallway. We gathered in the quiet and set a digital recorder and REM-Pod down. After some perfunctory questions, we replayed our session for review. At one point, a friend asked, "What's your name?" On playback, as clear as day, we all heard: "Frank." He didn't sound thrilled. But I was shocked to get such a clear response.

Around the time we were reviewing, I thought I felt something to my left side as I gently leaned against the wall, but it was one of those fleeting moments in an investigation that was so quick it didn't merit mentioning to the group at large. I mention it here, as any experience that matches up with simultaneous evidence is always interesting, even if only in retrospect. We didn't get much follow-up from "Frank" following the EVP, but I filed the name away for future investigations.

A little while later, we investigated the main meeting area in the building, where Elks members hold their gatherings. We sat in a large circle around the little dais in the center and read aloud through some of the Lodge material. A friend was using an *Ovilus*, hoping for meaningful responses to a series of questions. A few interesting words came through here and there, but when a few minutes later, my daughter's unique name appeared on-screen, I was a little unnerved. Coincidence though it may be, and though no further related responses came through, it was odd to see.

When I originally accepted my friend's invitation to investigate the Elks Lodge, my main excitement was being able to spend time in a haunted bowling alley. This unique room, with a bar at the back, was a fun space in which to set up equipment and attempt contact. How often are you encouraged to sit down in the middle of a bowling lane? The first visit did not yield much activity of note, but on my second visit to the Lodge, however, the unusual room finally gave me an unusual moment.

I was once again sitting on the slippery, polished floor of the bowling lane with the stairwell at my back. Our group had been seated awhile in the quiet darkness, some on the lanes with me, and some in chairs in the bar area. Things had been quiet, almost dull, for a while, and I was about to suggest moving rooms, when I heard the unmistakable hustle of someone running up or down the stairs. All members of our group were seated with us, except the Elks member hosting us, whom we'd left sitting quietly and contentedly in the upstairs bar. The sound of footsteps and creaking stair treads was so loud and obvious, at first I didn't even mark it as paranormal – I assumed someone had left for the restroom without my noticing. But when I acknowledged them to the group to "tag" them on the digital recorders, everyone confirmed no one had moved. One of my friends said she had heard that exact sound on her last visit to the Lodge.

I shot up from my seated position and bounded up the stairs – surely the Elks member was moving up the stairs to get something from another room – but no, he was still seated at the bar, watching a baseball game on mute. He'd hosted enough paranormal evenings at the Lodge to know full well he needed to keep still so as not to disturb the group on the property. He looked surprised to see me when I burst in the room. I lifted my hand in a quick wave, surely a confused look on my face to mirror his own puzzled expression. I was stumped. I spun around and parked myself on the stairwell landing above the bowling alley, hoping to hear a reprise, but heard nothing more. Darn it.

And that's how a lot of nights go – there might be a flurry of activity or sporadic small bits for a while and then nothing the rest of the night. Conversely, there may be absolutely nothing – until you're packing up your gear and things start going crazy. You may experience audio phenomena one evening and a visual anomaly the following visit. Patience is the name of the game. It's invaluable to return to the same location to gather data over multiple evenings – ghosts do not perform on cue, and one night is hardly enough time to truly get the feel of activity somewhere. These were people, after all – they may need to get accustomed to you before they decide to interact. I have been fortunate in my paranormal career to return to several locations frequently and thus compile and compare findings from one investigation to the next. Another location I have visited multiple times, and one I don't think I'll ever fully be done visiting, is Pennhurst State School.

CHAPTER 15

PENNHURST STATE SCHOOL AND HOSPITAL

SPRING CITY, PENNSYLVANIA

There are some haunted locations that are on everyone's bucket lists, and my home turf just outside Philadelphia is situated within easy distance from a few of these well-known haunted spots. I am lucky enough to live about ten minutes from one of the behemoths of the paranormal world – Pennhurst State School.

Pennhurst is often mistakenly called Pennhurst Asylum – an unfortunate moniker derived from the haunted house attraction that is run in October at Pennhurst and features actors dressed as undead patients and doctors jumping out at visitors for a scary seasonal thrill. As much as I love Halloween, this just never sits right with me; Pennhurst's history is just too tragic.

The facility was originally known as the *Eastern Pennsylvania Institution for the Feeble-Minded and Epileptic,* and once upon a time was seen as a model institution for mental health care, which, as we know by now, is not saying much for the 1900s. Since the eighteenth century, people with illnesses and disabilities were labeled "defectives," and "treatment" of varying levels of inefficacy were performed at the lowest cost possible. While written history shows that many compassionate nurses and volunteers did their best to care for residents, in the end, without adequate funding or attention from the state, residents at Pennhurst were treated abysmally. One ghastly example is the common practice of tooth removal to discourage "bad" behavior. Pennhurst is now often referred to as "the Shame of Pennsylvania."[14]

On May 30, 1974, the mother of a resident filed the landmark civil rights case *Halderman v. Pennhurst State*, which eventually reached the United States Supreme Court. The facts brought out in this case plainly illustrated the horrific conditions lack of funding created at Pennhurst. The judge claimed, "It was only through the dedication of the overworked staff, it seems, that any humanity at all was afforded in this institution."[15]

In 1984, Pennhurst was closed by the judge's orders, its residents dispersed either to other institutions or simply deposited into the nearest town. In the years since, Pennhurst's ownership has been in the crosshairs of many bidding wars after portions of the grounds were repurposed as a residential home for veterans. Another portion of the upper campus was turned over to the PA National Guard for use as an armory. In 2016, many buildings were in such a state of severe decay that they were demolished. Pennhurst is currently privately owned, and bookings for daytime history tours, photography tours, and overnight paranormal investigations have become increasingly popular since the site's appearance on several popular paranormal TV programs. There is an ever-lingering threat to demolish more buildings as they decay to unsafe conditions, much to the anguish of paranormal enthusiasts who yearn to visit.

I have visited Pennhurst several times, and when I drive

anywhere in the vicinity of the sprawling campus, I inevitably crane my neck to try to catch a glimpse through the surrounding tangles of trees. Though the facility is massive, it is well concealed from prying eyes like mine by large forest clumps bordering the fields around the buildings of interest.

My first true visit to Pennhurst, where I strolled the grounds, mouth agape in awe, was to attend the 2019 Paranormal Convention that started it all for me. I didn't know when I woke that day, excited to attend the event, that it would change the direction of everything for me going forward. A blazing heat wave had hit the area that morning, and sweat slid down my back as they fastened my paper daily pass bracelet onto my wrist. If I had to drag myself on my knees over the broken cement walkways, keeled over from heat exhaustion, I wasn't leaving before I'd drunk my fill of that spooky day.

It was at that convention that I unwittingly walked right by vendor tables hosted by people who would be my friends in the future, where I stood outside the Mayflower building and got full-body shivers gazing up at the decaying window casements above. I was captivated by the eerie playground in the main square, with a child's slide being slowly devoured by winding tendrils of weeds. I perused the vendors' area, which was probably topping 102 degrees under a giant black tent, purchasing various handmade items and chatting with investigative teams, before sitting for a few wonderful lectures outside. I was thrilled to chat with a few of my favorite TV investigators and snap some photos, but looking back, I wish I had taken the opportunity to investigate with them that night. I got my chance at Pennhurst, eventually.

I have been on two investigation nights at Pennhurst so far, the first of which as a true novice – only the second of all my investigation evenings ever. It was a public event, meaning anyone interested could purchase a ticket, at any level of experience, and be led through the location by a seasoned team. It was set up so a tour guide would allow you into a building, where you could borrow equipment and try your hand at connecting with spirits. In the end, my guides that night were more interested in smoking cigarettes outside rather than investigating alongside the group, but as it happened, that gave me and my friend a little more freedom in deciding where we went.

I loved entering the gloom of one of the most famous haunted properties in Pennsylvania, with dusty stairwells and endless graffiti on every wall in sight; it was like Disneyland to me. Some buildings at Pennhurst are so decayed that visitors can no longer enter them for fear of falling right through the floor; you can only admire them from afar. When our tour guide wrapped up her opening lines for the evening and wandered outside, I broke off from the group with my friend at my side, dashing to the highest floor to get some space from the more raucous tour-goers, to try our hand at connecting with Pennhurst ghosts. We found an old bathroom in one of the dormitory buildings and decided we'd set up shop to begin. I set down my video camera, pointing towards us, fired up a dim ambient light cube I felt rather clever for finding on Amazon in the "children's décor" section, and sat in the quiet.

If I compare my preferred investigation style then to now, the only major shift has been in my confidence and debunking skill set. Though I feel more comfortable with equipment and being present in a dark and quiet room, I still prefer to sit and let a location speak to me organically. I don't run in and demand communication from unseen residents, nor do I often launch right into questioning or even an Estes session. Introducing yourself by name, sitting in the quiet at a haunted site, and taking time to purposefully open your senses without equipment has become so underrated. Especially in locations with a tragic history, I have found this technique to be a respectful way to begin, to let the spirits get comfortable with my presence, and vice versa.

In that first visit to Pennhurst, the group was simply too large and too inexperienced to really trust anything we saw or heard. A long, dark hallway, lit only by a red Exit sign at the end, will always give me the creeps, but it's hard to stay in the moment when some of the group is cracking jokes and not-so-sneakily sneaking sips from flasks all around you. I love having fun and don't mind being silly on investigations; in fact, there are times I've even gotten more ghostly activity in that way, but there's an appropriate time for it. I hope I never seem like I consider myself "above" certain behavior, but surely there is a level of investigation etiquette in speaking to the dead, even at a public event.

The Pennhurst tunnel system, which runs the length of the campus, connecting many of the buildings when it was operational, is also said to be notoriously haunted. Our guide briefly brought us to the tunnels, but their innate structure causes severe echoing, even from whispers, and such a large group in such a space wasn't ideal. My tour guides got very excited about some hits I got on my K2 meter, but even back then I just didn't get overly excited about a K2 hit – there are just too many ordinary reasons for EMF levels to spike randomly. I still use a K2 meter, but it is always a secondary device, its activity only truly interesting if it spikes in tandem with another piece of equipment or coincides with a personal experience.

Public events are a great way to dip a toe into the world of investigating but invariably a little frustrating. I understand that a public event holds no candle to a private event – but again, the costs of booking a private night at a place like Pennhurst does not make for a cheap date. So, because I had not yet won the lottery, my second foray into investigating Pennhurst a year later was also a public event, though this round was a far better experience compared to my first. The guides on this visit, though long-winded on the history tour, were far more competent. The main group was broken down into smaller groups, who were then left to investigate different buildings in one-hour increments. So, my friend and I, plus a nervous friend on her first investigation, were able to set up actual experiments and get to know the space a little better without contamination from others. We ran a Spirit Box session in Mayflower, the building that housed nonverbal patients, and received a possible grunting EVP, and our REM-Pod went off in the doorway of one of the dorms on a higher level.

In the same building, as we sat in the common area of the residents' building, strips of paint peeling from the walls around us, my first-timer friend and I both saw a glimmer of light in the right corner across from us. Initially I thought it was a brief flash of light filtering through the ripped curtains fluttering in the humid breeze, but after jumping up from my seat to measure where the light hit, I saw that it couldn't have been what it was. I think as we sat in those worn seats, the partial cubicle wall looming at our backs, we witnessed a manifestation attempt by a nearby curious spirit. I had my video camera facing us from that corner, not toward it, and though I hoped perhaps I caught at least a glimpse of the light beside the camera, there was nothing. I was glad for the validation of my friend seeing it too.

Our most interesting session of the night was in the Devon building, which holds many of the medical offices on-site, as well as the isolation chambers upstairs, where unruly patients were sent to "cool off." We, of course, took the opportunity to shut ourselves into one of these isolation rooms, to my skittish first-timer friend's horror. My friend, using a thermal imaging device, was able to track a ten-degree temperature change in the room. We all felt the cold spot moving past us. I set a REM-Pod in a corner and began asking questions of the spirit. Many responses seemed to work in tandem with my line of questioning in the room. Nearby cat balls blinked as if in confirmation of the beeps and lights coming from the REM-Pod. It was my first time in the Devon building, and I was impressed by its activity.

Being closed into that small room with very little air flow, you cannot help but step into the shoes of the patients who had to endure these conditions. Indeed, the entirety of Pennhurst at night forces you to think about the experiences of the patients and just how bad it had to be for the state to come in and close it down entirely. I feel the pull to continue investigating at Pennhurst, if only to keep connecting more pieces of the puzzle of who is really still there, and show them that they have not been forgotten.

CHAPTER 16

SAMUEL MILLER MANSION

COLUMBIA, PENNSYLVANIA

I t's amazing what we will willingly put our bodies through in the name of paranormal investigation. We will drive hours and hours on icy roads, to towns in the middle of nowhere, fueled by far too many energy drinks to stay up until the sun begins to rise, all for a glimpse of something "Other." I have been soaked with sweat in an old decaying hospital room, so hungry my stomach rumbles were confused with demon growls, and so tired I've fallen asleep and nearly drooled on a haunted couch in an ex-brothel. But notably, there was an investigation where I was so freezing cold, I legitimately worried I'd lose my toes while trying to capture an EVP. This bitterly cold, yet interesting location was the Samuel Miller Mansion.

The Samuel Miller Mansion, originally built in 1804 (and apparently without a working furnace since then), was once the home of Samuel Miller, but was purchased in 1811 by a bridge company, whose treasurer lived on the property. Between the late 1800s to early 1900s, the property was owned by a horse carriage and feed company, until the invention and subsequent popularity of the automobile made the use of carriages irrelevant. In the 1920s, the Baker Toy company took over the property and flourished there for nearly six decades. Since its closure, two printing companies have operated from the premises, the second of which currently owns the property.[16] I have heard time and again that the property was connected to the efforts of the Underground Railroad, though I haven't been able to link any tangible history to this claim. However, records of this secretive effort were obviously kept quiet, unlikely to be fully documented, so I'll take it with a grain of salt on the word of the rumor mill.

One freezing night in January, I was invited to a private event at the mansion by a friend. I arrived to find it was a boisterous crowd, mostly comprised of men, only a handful of whom I knew beforehand, and all investigators who had been active in the field far longer than myself. Though the rich history of the location's many lives is quite interesting, this was an investigation where in the end, my main takeaway was a lesson in paranormal culture. I look back on that night as a lesson on the social flow of an investigative group, and a reminder on listening to one's own gut in every situation.

The claims on this property center heavily on "transient spirit," in other words, it isn't always the same spirit haunting the location, but different energies moving through the space. The proprietor of the location mentioned on the initial tour that a certain mirror upstairs was indeed a "portal" for such spirit voyages, a concept with which I continually struggle, possibly because so many other haunted locations claim a similar feature.

PORTALS

The theory of portals seems to be a common one amongst haunted locations. The concept is that a certain physical location or item within a haunted location is an egress point for spirits. It is the entranceway that they come through from the Other side, and the exit point for their departure. Some claim there are portals straight to Hell, while others are simple doorways where the Veil is thinner and more easily passed through.

A portal is sometimes a mirror, like at the Samuel Miller Mansion. Sometimes it is a well (like at the famed Bobby Mackey's Music World in Kentucky, for example), or simply a general physical area, perhaps the area under a staircase or a spot on the wall.

Portals are often associated with hauntings of a transient nature, in that the same ghosts do not stay in the location, but pass through, resulting in unpredictable investigation experiences and evidence captures. The ghosts who haunt the location near a portal may not necessarily be associated with the history of the property at all. It is an especially common claim at supposedly haunted hotels, as if the spirits move through the location on their own schedule, like the guests in life did.

Sometimes there are stories in which a portal was closed (say, a well was filled in) or destroyed, which resulted in increased or changed paranormal activity. The working theory is that the spirits who came through, expecting to be able to leave, are now stuck and are displeased about it. This may cause a sudden increase in perceived activity, or cause the opposite and rid the location of spirit guests.

Regardless of whether the mirror at the Samuel Miller Mansion is a true portal, I quickly sensed that the evening ahead might not yield as much as I'd hoped. It was less the location itself as much as it was how I was feeling. I have found, time and again, that the number and energy of people on an investigation affect a night's experience even more than the potential spirits there. Whether it is a matter of the spirits feeling a connection and wanting to communicate with some, but not all, of the investigators present, or simply a human tendency to shut down when uncomfortable, I cannot definitively say. I can say, though, that for myself, when I am forced into close quarters with a personality that clashes too much with mine at a haunted site, I may as well pack my gear kit and head home for the night. I aim for flexibility in my views, especially regarding the paranormal. I don't always need a leadership role. But especially as a woman, there is such a thing as too far beyond a reasonable adjustment in an effort to "go with the flow."

In moving through many occasions of investigating alongside others who have been active in the field longer than I have (who are typically keen to tell me so), I have learned so much about not only ghosts, investigation styles, and other people, but myself. I know that I will always have more to learn. I haven't reached the end of my journey, which excites me. As we all should be, I am willing to accept constructive criticism, tips, and information passed to me in a respectful manner with pure intent. I've learned how to maneuver many personalities and belief systems in this field, and I've been impressed witnessing different investigation styles seamlessly blended without judgment by either side. I've seen one person use dowsing rods while another uses a REM-Pod simultaneously. Some like to sit quietly in a hotspot room while another will pull tarot cards during an EVP session. I've seen incredible teamwork lead to fascinating results.

I've quickly learned, however, that sometimes an initial eagerness to work together is not enough to get the job done. Overly confident males send my hackles up, and I tend to shut down, and this irritated state of mind inevitably prohibits the openness I know we all need when attempting to contact the Other side. I cannot come from a place of calm neutrality and willingness to communicate when I am forced on our session breaks to be regaled by stories of an individual's various minor television appearances, or subtly touched on my arm or back. I do not feel grounded and receptive when, during an EVP session, as I am trying to listen to tentative spirits, someone fills every silence with too many questions, assumptions, and demands of both the spirit and myself.

"Spirit, make yourself known."

Maybe they don't care for your demands. Maybe they need more time to respond and you're asking too many rapid-fire questions for them to keep up.

"Ask questions! Don't be so nervous."

I'm not shy, nor am I nervous; I'm trying to give the spirit a chance to speak. Quietude and active listening are so often steamrolled by noise and aggressive methods.

"Smile, the ghosts will think you're grumpy."

Actually, if the spirits can see us, they are probably watching how I'm reacting to *you* and understand my facial expressions exactly. Has telling a woman to smile ever gone well for any man, anywhere, ever?

I smirked at one man's shocked expression when I volunteered to go alone down the so-called "dark hallway" at the back of the building. In this brief moment of solitude (at least in regard to the living), I felt a slight touch of unseen fingers on my wrist after I said hello and asked a few questions. Was a spirit finally reaching out? It was too little time to lean into the moment or gather more information before the men came barreling in to join me.

I am a strong woman – a mother, a wife, a woman in a world where we must fight for the same respect men are naturally given. Softness is not weakness in life, and certainly not in paranormal investigation. I have never been a "hater of men"; I have too many excellent examples of male specimens in my life for that. But being flirtatiously teased by a man at an event or endlessly peppered with another investigator's bravado is distracting, disrespectful, and a complete waste of my time. The time away from my family that I set aside for investigating is precious. I no longer sacrifice my commodities – energy, time, money, opportunity for paranormal research – to the egos of loud men. There are many lovely male investigators in the community; it is a shame that they seem to be so few and far between, in my experience.

Along these lines is a lesson I wished I had learned on my very first minute of my very first outing into paranormal research: it is imperative to remain true to your own observations on an investigation and not get swept away in a group's collective excitement. It's important not to succumb to the influence of others and what they demand that they see, hear, or feel, no matter how badly you want to see, hear or feel something. Honesty is paramount above all else. Stay open, but stay reasonable, too.

For example, in my time at the Samuel Miller Mansion, I was alongside those who insisted they were seeing an obvious shadow figure five feet in front of me. I saw nothing, and I told them so. They insisted I was looking at the wrong spot. He walked to that spot, and lo and behold, he was standing where lights between the slats of the wide-planked floor above were being blocked out off-and-on by investigators we knew to be standing right above us. It was at that point I realized that nothing I said to refute this man's claims was going to get through his conviction. He was either too swept up in the moment and really believed it, or he didn't want to acknowledge he'd made a mistake. Granted, I've been in situations where I think I see or hear something, and when confronted with a plausible, non-paranormal truth dissolving my claim, I have felt momentarily deflated and minorly embarrassed. But it is our duty to abide by Occam's razor – the simplest explanation is probably the correct one – and look for the truly special experience. Acknowledging debunking errors along the way will only enrich the experience of having that real, truly unexplainable moment when it happens.

I did have one memorably interesting moment that night, though unfortunately it was by way of a digital application, in which I don't place a lot of trust. Towards the end of the evening, my friend and I were sitting on the floor with some children's toys in front of us, while a man in the group ran an app on his laptop. It would occasionally blurt out indecipherable sounds and partial words, all in voices that came with the app itself. The man asked questions, and we listened to the garbled sounds, my faith in the device waning further. Then, as the man asked, "Do you remember my name?" A moment later, the voice said his name, each syllable clearly heard. He whirled around with an excited gasp, yelling to the rest of the groups throughout the building. I definitely heard it, and it was definitely memorable, but I'm still on the fence as to its supernatural origins. It was his laptop, after all. Then again, maybe my headspace was too suspicious and crabby from oppressive energy to take anything in and believe it by that point.

So, another investigation on the tally, teaching me another lesson of what I want from my paranormal journey, and what I don't. I'm grateful for each spooky night, however things pan out. Hauntings are as unique as the individuals walking this planet, and someone's experience at a haunted location can often come down to how well a location and its spirits connect to an individual investigator. For some people, battlefields speak; for others, decrepit asylums whisper their ghostly secrets in one's ear and not another's.

The "Holy Grail" is evidence or a shared experience that everyone can see, hear, or feel, and no one can definitively dispute, but then again, there are just some cases that hit you in your gut. You can step foot inside a location, and there is a Knowing in your bones by physically being there, even if the rest of your group is unaffected. Collective group hysteria is one thing; quiet certainty is another. The entire reason I dove into the field was for this feeling, for those profound moments and feelings that cannot be captured and shared. So far, nowhere in my paranormal journey has affected me as much in this way as my time at the Shanley Hotel.

CHAPTER 17

THE SHANLEY HOTEL

NAPANOCH, NEW YORK

O n my visit to a small hotel in upstate New York, I had finally, *finally* seen a full-body, nontransparent apparition. After I chased the figure I'd seen into the gentlemen's club room and found nothing, I felt dumbstruck. I slowly walked out from the hallway with what I'm told was a comically shocked expression on my face, as white as the ghost I had seen. My brain would not stop replaying the previous few minutes, still searching for clues to the truth. I replayed it, step by step: my friend leaned down, a bustling figure quickly moved across the hallway, left to right, as if originating from the mirror scrying room.

MIRROR SCRYING

Scrying is a form of divination in which one looks onto a reflective surface such as water, or glass to see visual cues for spirit information. Sometimes fire gazing is implemented to the same end. In an even more subjective version, some might scatter eggshells, cleaned bones, or stones and interpret the pattern in which they land. The viewer in any case subjectively interprets what they see to conclude what messages or symbols are meant to be relayed by spirit.

Scrying with a reflective surface can also be thought to simply offer a neutral place for the eye to rest and enhance a meditative state, helping the participant tune into their other senses and receive messages through their "third eye." Mirror scrying is, obviously, using a mirror to engage in scrying; often the mirror is painted black. Scrying is a highly subjective technique and does not supply much in the way of shareable evidence, as the message relies on the participant's description alone. Some consider that the message relayed is meant for the recipient alone, connected by myriad subtleties in that moment to the spirit.

~

At the moment I saw the figure, some rapid-fire thoughts moved swiftly through my rattled brain: it was very tall, uncommonly so; had it been floating? It didn't seem to care one bit that we were there or what we were doing, it didn't even look at us – because it didn't have a head, I suddenly recalled. Above either a well-endowed chest or a ruffled collar was nothing. It wasn't gruesome; there was just nothing much above the shoulder area except a small wispy mass just above the swell at the top of the torso. Its behavior made me wonder if it was a residual spirit. If it didn't have a head to see us with, it couldn't be intelligent, right? But if it didn't have a head, how did the body move?

In theory, if a spirit is residual, it is either replaying an emotionally impactful moment or event, or it is replaying an action that was done so many times in life, the spirit continues repeating it after death. Maybe a residual spirit is using some ethereal version of "muscle memory" in repeating these motions. Is a mind-body interaction irrelevant posthumously? I mean, really, why would a spirit expend extra energy to manifest unnecessary body parts? My thoughts were a whirlwind, though I'm sure in reality, it was all in just a few seconds as I propelled myself toward the point it had disappeared. All these thoughts and more bounced around my shocked brain as I tried to come back to the present moment and competently, calmly relay the events to the group around me. Later that night I sent a simple text to my cousin in Colorado: "Hey. So, ghosts are real." This hotel had just blown my mind.

Before it was a popular hotel and speakeasy owned by James Shanley in the 1920s, the Shanley Hotel was a family home that saw more than its fair share of tragedy, including the death of a three-year-old girl, Rosie, who fell down a well on the property, and a son of the house, called Jonathan, accidentally run over by his father's car. At the height of the bootlegging operation running there during the Prohibition era, the property also housed a gentlemen's club and upstairs bordello, the ladies bustling down the narrow staircase to lure men to their carnal delights in the rooms above. It was in this area of the hotel where I witnessed my apparition. Perhaps the apparition I saw that night at the Shanley was a lady of the night or the madam in charge, briskly moving through the hallway to speak with a gentleman, as she had done countless times in life.

The hotel fell into disrepair after it closed down in 1991 and sat vacant for many years. When it was eventually purchased in 2005 by an individual keen to restore it to its former glory, it wasn't long before he started to have paranormal experiences there. He opened the hotel for overnight paranormal investigations in 2007.[17] This much-beloved owner passed away (and is thought by some to have joined the rank of Shanley spirits at the location), and the hotel is now owned by individuals who have volunteered on the property for many years. The building's lively history, rich in both scandalous and tragic tales, has made this space near and dear to many paranormal enthusiasts' hearts in the years since. I now include myself in the throngs of those fascinated by the activity at this location, and not only for the apparition I saw that night.

Most visitors are particularly enthralled with the story of little Rosie, who died in the well. Rosie's father was the barber on-site at the hotel, and he and his family lived in the side of the building that is now referred to as the bordello and gentlemen's club, after its function in the years after the family's residency. One of the bedrooms there now is in fact called "Rosie's Room." One day while playing near the well on the property, she fell in, hitting her head on the way down and falling to her death. In their grief, unable to withstand seeing the well from their residence every day, her family moved away. But it would seem to some that the spirit of little Rosie stayed behind.

When I visited the Shanley, I admit that I had little desire to seek Rosie out. I feel guilty saying this, especially as a mother, but it was *because* I am a mother that I could not bear to find evidence of a child ghost "stuck" anywhere. I feel selfish shame in my desire to distance myself from this claim, and feel that because I have children myself, I should have been keen to reach out to a child spirit, if I could offer her any comfort at all. In the end, I believe a child spirit found me and recognized, somehow, that I am a mother.

Towards the end of our evening, we went upstairs to the bordello to run a double Estes session, meaning there were two investigators "under," or wearing noise-cancelling headphones listening to the scanning stations, while others asked questions just outside in the attached parlor area. The listeners simply say out loud what words, phrases, or noises they hear, while the rest of the group asks questions, hoping a mean-ingful response will line up. Up until this evening, I enjoyed casual listening to the Spirit Box, hoping to hear something impressive, but I'd only really heard quick syllables or one-word moments obviously from local radio stations. The Shanley seemed determined to disabuse me of some of my preconceived notions that evening.

Perched on the bed in the room next to Rosie's Room, I took my turn listening to the SB-7 with a blindfold on, while the sessions livestreamed on social media. I sat, tried not to fidget, and settled into the rhythm of the white noise alternating with the usual bits of short, clipped words. After a few minutes, I started to hear two distinct female voices come forward, picking up the pace in responses. They sounded vaguely argu-mentative or taunting of each other, and I imagined in my mind's eye, given my surroundings, that they were two former ladies of the night discussing their usual work. It was interest-ing, but there was still nothing that really stuck out as definitive (apart from a moment in which they seemed to joke about how much they would charge to service the male friends who were sitting with us. The responses implied that they'd be charging a bigger fee than usual, poor guys). As the responses of these female voices faded away, there was a period of rela-tive quiet. All of a sudden, crystal clear, heard over multiple seconds of the rhythmic "shush" noises of the scanning beneath, I heard a child's voice call out, "I can't, Mommy!" in a panicked tremor. I still get goosebumps when I recall that sweet voice.

I couldn't help but gasp in shock and clutch my chest. I had never heard such a lengthy, emotive, clear voice come through the Spirit Box before. My heartbeat was in my ears as I listened intently for any other words in the same voice, but none came. I was shaken up by this second major experience in a short span of time – keep in mind this occurred within hours of my seeing a full-body apparition for the first time. I was mildly irked no one had heard the voice because it was in my headphones, as no one had seen the figure either, and I'm sure I seemed jumpy and a bit dramatic to the rest of the group by this point. While I've since tried to rationally debunk it, and considered whether the response was feasibly a voice caught from a local baby monitor, I'm stubbornly holding my ground on this one. It wouldn't hold up in any imaginary "paranormal evidence courtroom," but it truly felt like this was another moment of being singled out by the entities on the property, for better or worse.

$$\sim$$

After the Estes sessions wrapped up, I was emotionally and physically exhausted. I like to joke that I was drained by the spirits in the hotel for their manifestations, and I'm only partly in jest – after all, I seemed to be the only one experiencing significant phenomena, and I was the one losing steam the fastest. The day's events just caught up to me. I did my best and stayed half-awake and semi-coherent for a final EVP session up on the third floor, but around 1 a.m. I had to tap out and go to bed. Luckily, a close friend was there that night who was exhausted too. We claimed "the Rose Room" with two beds, and I was asleep, still fully clothed, in minutes.

An hour or two later, I was awakened by footsteps entering the room, though I hadn't heard the rickety door open. The wooden floorboards creaked with their distinctive sound as the steps moved in a slow but steady line toward my bed, closer and closer. I awoke but refused to open my eyes, my thin blanket pulled up over my ears as I faced the wall next to my bed. I briefly thought the footsteps belonged to our other friend, who had stayed up later and was just finishing for the night, but I somehow knew it wasn't her. I breathed as quietly as I could, my heart rate quickening, as I heard the footsteps approach my bed. Whoever it was now stood directly behind my back as I lay on my side in the single bed along the wall. I felt a slight pressure on the side of the bed, as if someone was leaning over me. Without any reason why, I distinctly remember feeling "they" knew I was awake and purposely not opening my eyes, and found it mildly entertaining. I kept my eyes shut tight, both out of cold fear, and part out of exasperation, to be honest. This entity had literally eight hours in which it could have made itself known directly. I was a mother, I was tired, and I was done with ghostly shenanigans for the day. I retrospectively joke now, but in that moment, I was afraid. After a few moments, the footsteps receded, I know not where.

I was grateful for my exhaustion, as I was able to fall back to sleep shortly after that final encounter. As the first rays of sunlight hit my pillow, I drifted up to consciousness and spun around in my bed. I half-expected to see the ghost still standing beside me, but I saw only the bundled-up singular form of my friend. I did not see the other friend whom I had thought came in later. I'd find out later she indeed had slept elsewhere, never having stepped foot in the Rose Room that night. As quietly as I could, a purpose quickly defeated by the creaking floor, I stood and made my way to the bathroom to brush my teeth and change clothing for the long ride home. I warily eyed the spaces behind me in the bathroom mirror as I tidied up, but saw nothing.

As I opened the bathroom door, my friend's eyes were open; she looked exhausted. I apologized for waking her and shuffled back to plop down on the pile of blankets on my bed, not quite ready to be fully awake just yet. She sat up, and her first words to me were, "Did you hear those footsteps?"

I was equally grateful and terrified that I had some validation, even just for that one experience. She added that she hadn't fallen asleep before she heard them, feeling too nervous to sleep in a haunted hotel – and she confirmed that she saw no body belonging to the steps, but heard them as clear as day. Not only that, but she even felt someone sit on her bed shortly thereafter. I cannot speak to her experience in any detail, but our room definitely seemed to be an overnight hotspot. The rest of the group, spread out amongst other rooms in the main building with us and in the gentlemen's room under the bordello, heard a few bumps in the night, but nothing nearly as disarming.

This one single night in April 2021 at the Shanley Hotel held three of the most intense paranormal experiences I've ever had, yet no one else in my group had picked up on very much at all. Why? In the time since that visit, I've wondered whether sometimes one investigator's energy just syncs up better than others with a location, for one reason or another. Sometimes, locations feel like they're reaching out very specifically to individuals, when the rest of us just look on and subtly shrug.

It's another example to emphasize that trust amongst your investigation group is so vital – anyone can exaggerate or even full-out lie about their experiences; unfortunately, we see it time and time again in this field. I've consistently found it best to keep your investigation group small, and even better if you can spend time together bonding a little before you dive into investigation mode. The trust has to be there. Only when we are in a situation in which we feel safe and grounded can we really receive the message the spirits want to communicate.

CHAPTER 18

INN AT HERR RIDGE AND DEVIL'S DEN ON THE BATTLEFIELD

GETTYSBURG, PENNSYLVANIA

I made my way to Gettysburg, Pennsylvania, early one November afternoon after a treacherous two-hour drive in the pelting, freezing rain. I'd spent the drive earnestly listening to Christmas songs to distract myself from my white-knuckled grip on the steering wheel, my windshield wipers on full blast. I finally arrived as the rain eased off, and as I made my way through the charming town to the haunted inn I'd booked with my friend, the battlefield suddenly opened up on either side of the road. The wooden split-rail fences with open fields beyond, dotted with artillery, are such a strong visual it just takes your breath away. Our plans were jam-packed into one afternoon and evening, not nearly enough time for such a veritable goldmine of a haunted town, but we were trying to make do with what time we could fit into our schedules. It was times like this I wished I had jumped into my paranormal research much earlier in life, before marriage and children, when my days were my own to travel and leisurely explore. But timing is everything, as they say.

We had planned for multiple stops around town on our

trip. So once we were checked in to our inn, I set up an abandonment session in our shared room before we headed out to our other activities.

ABANDONMENT SESSIONS AND TRIGGER OBJECTS

An abandonment session is my favorite way to start any investigation. The idea is simple – literally set up a video camera, aimed toward a hotspot according to the claims on the property, and go about your business elsewhere. I often drop some cat balls, a K2 meter, and a REM-Pod if I have one, in the frame as well. In many cases, I am not actively rolling my second video camera as I go about the night, because I am in the moment and focused on an experiment like an Estes or EVP session. It's ideal to focus on the activity at hand and not be constantly distracted by the need to record and film, but having footage to review later is half the fun. With a passive abandonment session rolling, there is an extra set of "eyes" at all times while you are free to focus on the moment at hand. Sometimes, it may even be that a spirit is too shy to interact directly, and a lone camera may pick up a spirit who prefers an empty room.

In addition to a smattering of equipment, I almost always set up an abandonment session with trigger objects, items meant to entice spirit interaction. These may be items from the general time period of the spirit thought to be present, food or drink offerings, or even cigarettes or handcuffs, depending on where you are and what might rile up activity. Finding an item that actually belonged to the spirit thought to be present is ideal, though rare.

If a location has claims of both adult and child spirits, I like to set up separate trigger object piles. The pile intended for adults often includes alcohol, jewelry, and/or playing cards, while in the children's setup I usually place candy and small toys. Investigators themselves can sometimes even act as the trigger object; I have, on occasion, played music from the general era to try to encourage comfort and familiarity for the spirit, hoping they engage. If I happened to look a little silly doing the Charleston on the bowling alley lane of an old Elks Lodge, then so be it. Hopefully the ghosts had a good laugh at my expense; I don't mind. Some people will dress up in period clothes and speak only in the language style of the time, avoiding current slang that might confuse a decades-old ghost.

There are many nuances to the concept of using trigger objects while investigating. I find it fascinating and an experiment style with endless untapped potential for extraordinary results.

The abandonment session I set up at the inn was aimed toward the closet to the side of the bed, with the bedspread partially in view. Unbeknownst to us, the footage from this setup would later be very interesting indeed, capturing unexplainable sounds coming from inside the room. However, our dedicated investigation of the inn and its fascinating claims would come later – first we wanted to grab a fortifying meal and head to experience the battlefield while we still had daylight left. It was Veteran's Day, it was raining, and we were investigating the Gettysburg Battlefield at dusk.

DEVIL'S DEN

The history of Gettysburg and its significance in the Civil War is universally well known in America; the epic clash that took place there has inspired countless essays, books, films, and more. Gettysburg claims the title of the Civil War's bloodiest battle and was the turning point for the Union Army, shaping the United States as it is today. In the paranormal world, Gettysburg is a dream destination; the entire town is dotted with haunted locations. The battlefield itself is supposedly teeming with spirits, both residual and intelligent, and most enthusiasts cannot wait to explore it for themselves. The Parks Department does not allow after-hours investigations of the battlefield, so on my visit, we entered the gates as close to closing time as we could, to lose a bit of the light and explore at dusk. The field is vast, and it can be overwhelming to pinpoint a specific focal area, but you really can't go wrong. However, I was anxious to see and investigate Devil's Den, a boulder-strewn battle site that witnessed a brutal fight between Confederate and Union armies in 1863. It is a known hotspot for a great many paranormal claims, including full-body apparitions; that was our target area.

Devil's Den is easily recognizable by its large rock forma-tions scattered across the landscape, creating unique crevices and hidden stone bunkers in contrast to the majority of the flat battlefield nearby. Most of these formations are comprised of a dark igneous rock called diabase, which runs under a majority of the park, but is prominently evident in Devil's Den from extensive weathering over the years. (As an aside, diabase is not a rock type commonly associated with Stone Tape theory, as described previously.) The name Devil's Den originates from the nineteenth century, when locals thought a large, vicious snake lived inside the crevice in the center of the area. In all likelihood, there may have been.

At the time of the Civil War, the rocks of Devil's Den provided some cover and strategic defensive positions for the soldiers. However, the expanse of the diabase rock across the area made it impossible for troops to dig in and create cover for themselves as they usually did, so they were forced to scramble for a new strategy if their position was unsuitable. Subsequently, they had to rely on existing outcrops of rock and boulders for protection. Because of the Union Army's inability to build protective trench defenses, they suffered heavy losses of twenty-three thousand men, despite being declared victorious in the end. The attacking Confederates lost more than twenty-eight thousand men, which equated to more than a third of the entire Confederate Army.[18,19,20]

While the area's bloody clash is infamous to any history buff, and the area's rock formations are of great interest to geologists, Devil's Den has been notorious for its paranormal claims for many years. The site was legendary even before the Civil War; legends from the local Native American Susquehannock tribe whispered of hauntings at Devil's Den long before the Civil War era. Despite older ghost stories, the particularly compelling claims are the many eyewitness accounts of seeing Texan soldiers wandering near the precariously towering stone formations. Some of the more fantastic accounts include spirits intelligent and coherent enough to offer helpful directions to lost visitors seeking the way back to the walking path.

On my visit, by the time my friend parked her car and we headed across the small lot towards Devil's Den, the pelting rain from earlier in the day had lessened somewhat, though it was still drizzling. The ground was soggy and thick with mud in many places; the uneven stone paths were dangerously slippery. We had perhaps an hour or two to explore, probably less with the failing late-autumn light, so we wasted no time in making our way up the hill. I was a little ahead of my friend, moving up the path to the top of the hill, and I was starting to feel uneasy. The grip on my umbrella slipped in my increasingly cold fingers as the misting rain picked up. I turned to say something to my friend, and it was at this point that she turned to me, her face pale. She claimed to have glimpsed something that rattled her, unseen by me.

TIME SLIP PHENOMENA

One of the strangest paranormal theories to digest, and one of the most fascinating, is time slip phenomena. This is one of those topics that is so wonderfully weird and engaging that a short blurb to explain it is almost offensively inadequate, but will have to suffice. It is the idea that we are not actually always experiencing ghosts as the souls or remnants of deceased people, but instead, we are catching a glance of a different time period. It begins with channeling your inner Stephen Hawking and considering time as nonlinear. Time slip phenomena is almost as though a piece of cloth, representing the timeline, is folded or wrinkled temporarily, and two pieces of the same cloth meet briefly. At this meeting point, the moments of time intersect in the same general geography, and individuals in both time periods can experience each other.[21]

If you subscribe to this theory, you are open to the idea that to see a ghost is to actually see through a brief rip in time; you are looking at a living person on a different plane of time. You may even see or hear yourself, younger or older than your current age.[22] Similarly, some variations on this theory dictate that we are seeing through a rip not in time, but in dimensions, glimpsing a different dimension that usually invisibly co-exists with ours. It's a mind-bender for sure. At any rate, it's been suggested that this is a phenomenon that envelops Gettysburg, fueling its many ghost stories and supernatural claims.

~

A fter documenting the area beside the path, but not experiencing anything more except the biting cold of the quickly plummeting temperature, we continued moving up to the top of the hill. As we reached the plateau at the top, I had an overwhelming sense of wanting to dash back to the car as quickly as possible, which is unlike me. The thought of wasting the precious time I'd set aside for this trip was abhorrent to me and kept me from turning tail and running for the relative safety of the car. However determined I was, my slick-soled boots were no match for climbing over some of the larger boulders, and my sense that something was wrong, that something was watching us, was putting me off-balance mentally. We wandered a bit, taking photos of the few monuments and the stark silhouette of the tall tree growing there, calling a furtive greeting to the spirits we hoped were around us. Unfortunately, between the rain and creeping darkness of evening, we couldn't see much of the battlefield area of Little Round Top that we knew stretched out before us. And all this time, my heart rate was fast in my chest; I just felt unsafe, somehow. My body couldn't seem to discern between an immediate threat, or if there was something of a paranormal origin settling around us. My gut was telling me something was afoot.

I was straining my ears to hear the phantom cannon fire I'd heard about, but instead, my friend and I both suddenly heard a distant groan or yell from somewhere behind us. We jumped and turned to each other, confirming we each had heard it. However, a car on its way toward the park exit had driven past us a few minutes prior, so we chalked it up to living human noise, probably intentionally frightening us as a joke. We had probably given them a fright ourselves as they passed – two women suddenly looming out of the darkness in the rain. A pair of weirdos, to be sure. Apart from our fellow tourists, we also knew from our research that the ridges on either side of the Military Park, plus the hard rock formations throughout Devil's Den, can create sound echoes. But given everything else I was feeling at the time, I still vaguely wonder if I was too quick to dismiss the eerie sound. Perhaps it was related to my unease after all.

As it grew even darker, my discomfort crept closer to mild panic, and we decided to walk down and around on the car path back to the parking lot, instead of trying to blindly navigate down the wet stones we had climbed up. As we walked, my friend suddenly stopped just in front and slightly to the right of me, mumbling to herself that she had just seen something crawl across the road. I immediately lifted my phone, which was already open to my camera, and tried to snap a fast photo. At that point, to my shock, my phone completely froze, with an error message I had never seen before nor since displayed on the screen. I broke out in a cold chill as I tried again and again to take a photo, but my phone camera would not yield. I was shocked – camera malfunction in the presence of spirit activity was one of the exact claims said to occur at this location. It was one of those claims that I had flippantly dismissed when I heard it, and here it was, staring me in the face. Serves me right.

When it comes to technology and the paranormal, I feel the same as when my college roommate's computer mysteriously turned itself on in the middle of the night – suspicious that it may have just been some kind of glitch or power surge that I don't understand because I am not an electrician or engineer. Not every technological malfunction is paranormal. I've questioned if certain types of rocks, like diabase, can affect cell phone performance. While many studies exist on how cell phone *signal* strength can be affected by such things, I found nothing correlating local geology and the malfunction of a phone's offline internal applications. All in all, despite unknown technical factors, if two eerie experiences occur simultaneously, the event seems more meaningful. In this case in Gettysburg, my extreme unease before the camera error, paired with my friend's visual claim, all merge to establish a compelling paranormal event.

That night, after a few minutes, I gave up trying to get my camera to work and set my phone to restart. I peered at the path ahead, seeing nothing unusual, to my disappointment. My friend and I continued on our way to the car: cold, wet, vaguely nauseated, and absolutely puzzled at the flurry of activity we'd experienced in just that short amount of time. When we reached the car, my phone had finished restarting, and my camera worked perfectly. I filmed the road in front of us as we followed the path out of the park, hoping to catch an anomaly, but capturing only rain-soaked fields punctuated by the occasional memorial stone.

THE INN AT HERR RIDGE

My mind was still reeling from the intense experiences on the battlefield as we returned to the inn and changed into dry clothes. I scooped up the abandonment camera I had left running, ending that session and safely tucking the memory card away. I'd review the footage later at home. For the moment, it was time to settle in and fire up the investigation of our room at the haunted inn.

The building, which is now the Inn at Herr Ridge, was originally established in 1815, and it was used as a stop for the Underground Railroad. It remained a tavern until 1828 when it was purchased by Frederick Herr, who renamed it Herr Tavern and added lodging accommodations for guests. When the Civil

War broke out, the inn was used as a Confederate field hospital; its history from that period is rife with horrid tales of emergency amputations and gruesome battle injuries. It is unclear how many deaths occurred on the property, but it is well documented that hundreds of amputations occurred in what are now guest rooms 1, 2, and 3. Herr owned the tavern until his death in 1868, after which the tavern was bought and sold many times. In 1977, it was most recently purchased and restored into an inn and restaurant.[23]

The inn quickly garnered its haunted reputation, even being featured on paranormal television and online media through the years. I had been looking forward to experiencing all the claims this building had to offer, the list of which is considerable. Patrons at the bar claim feeling someone push against them but seeing no one nearby. Others tell of candles relighting minutes later, bottles moving by themselves on the bar, and hearing the moans of men coming through the walls. In room 1, a male spirit in soldier attire is commonly seen. In the room I booked in particular, a child spirit has been seen standing near the closet, and footsteps are often heard.

It was fascinating to flip through the guestbook in the room and note the various mentions of ghostly activity:

"... We were greeted by a young girl standing by the closet. She was dressed in a linen off-white dress nearly floor length. She disappeared through the closet door after a minute."

"We awoke to footsteps above our heads... and the presence of spirits who mulled around the bed."

"We had a lot of spirit interaction... especially in rooms 3 and 4..."

We began our study of the room and tried to debunk a few

of the claims right off the bat. As a scented-candle fanatic myself, I quickly dismissed the claim of candles relighting; that can occur in any regular candle with a wick in need of a trim, or one that has burned too long, with an overabundance of hot liquid wax pooled at the base. Likewise, the bottles moving on a bar can be explained naturally; just a little moisture from condensation underneath a container would enable it to slide easily. These circumstances may not explain away every occurrence, but it is enough of a conceivable reasoning to dismiss them as paranormal and focus on other claims. Unsurprisingly, I was most excited about the reports of seeing an apparition.

I set a video camera up at the far end of the room, facing the bed, letting it record the rest of the evening and overnight. I noted that any K2 hits in the room would likely be irrelevant – the air conditioning kicked on often enough, even in November, to send a current of cool air through the room at regular intervals, which activated the meter every time. We tried an EVP session, but with no noticeable interaction and our mounting exhaustion from our action-packed day, we surrendered to the pull of sleep. It seemed as though our focus for the inn investigation would be largely comprised of reviewing overnight infrared video footage later.

We were up and out on the road early, dashing back to our homes and motherly responsibilities. It was a midweek investigation, after all, and duty called. I gave myself a few days of my regular routine at home before diving into the video review from my trip. When I finally got a quiet moment to intently watch and listen to my recordings, I was shocked by a few things that were captured.

During the time we were out traipsing around Devil's Den, while the abandonment session rolled in our room, a few distinct sounds were recorded that seemed out of place. Notably, there was the telltale sound of a doorknob moving very close to the camera, though it is not visible in-frame. Presumably, it was the old-fashioned, rickety doorknob of the bathroom door, which was positioned behind and slightly to the left of the camera setup. The metallic turn and release sound was quite distinctive, and both the bathroom door and the main door to the room have the same old-fashioned knobs. A similar, though quieter sound can be heard again when we eventually re-entered the room ourselves.

The next interesting capture was another sound on the recording from early in the day. The room we stayed in at the Inn at Herr Ridge has old wooden floorboards that flex with a distinctive creak as they are stepped upon. At a point when no living person was in the room, these footstep sounds are clearly audible, getting louder as they approach the camera. Nothing was disturbed visually, but these sounds are unmistakable, and when I heard them on the footage, I wished I had reviewed the recording when I was still in the room to follow up.

The last interesting capture is a visual one, though I waffle back and forth as to whether it was paranormal in nature or not. Before we retired for the night, my friend and I had folded up a luggage rack and placed it at the foot of the bed we shared, directly adjacent to the closet where there have been claims of a child apparition. On reviewing the footage, I noted that my friend got up to use the restroom many times throughout the night, passing the rack each time. (Incidentally, this also provided an example of the aforementioned creaking wooden floorboards.) At no point throughout the night did she bump into or even graze the rack as she passed, nor was the rack resting on the bedframe at all.

About forty-five minutes after my friend returned to the bed for the final time before morning, the rack suddenly moves on its own. It slumps over, away from the closet, falling open slightly from its folded-up position, as if it had been nudged. When I first noted the movement, I nearly dismissed it – surely she bumped it at some point, and eventually the tension on its legs on the carpet gave way, and it opened slightly – but she never touched it. Would a slight vibration in the floor be enough of a catalyst for eventual movement forty-five minutes later? Maybe, but something doesn't quite add up. As I say, I am on the fence about the origin of the movement of the rack, but I have tucked that particular moment away under the heading of "possibly paranormal."

Looking back on the trip to Gettysburg, while I am grateful that I was able to make some time to investigate and explore, I wish I had more: more time, more energy, more activity. I wish I had reviewed my footage on the spot. I wish I'd gulped an energy drink and gone to investigate the bar area before I fell asleep. I wish I'd seen that child apparition. Call it the greed of a paranormal investigator on the hunt.

CHAPTER 19
ΛΛRON BURR HOUSE
NEW HOPE, PENNSYLVANIA

Unlike most televised paranormal programs these days, sometimes a "haunted" location yields very little in the way of spooky activity in reality. Whether it is just an unfortunately quiet night, or your energy is a mismatch for the spirits, sometimes a much-anticipated investigation ends up being just a regular night away. These nights, however, are important simply to have a comparison point with more active locations in your case log. They act as a control with which to compare experiences, test equipment, and learn more about historical locations and moments in time. And from a mother's perspective, in all honesty, a night away from responsibilities is never a night wasted.

The Aaron Burr House in New Hope, Pennsylvania, was never actually the official residence of infamous politician Aaron Burr, but rather the home of friends to whom he fled after fatally wounding Alexander Hamilton in the duel of July 11, 1804. When Alexander Hamilton died from his wounds, Aaron Burr was charged with murder in New York and New Jersey. In the interim, awaiting his fate, he initially stayed at what is now the Aaron Burr House before fleeing to South Carolina to stay with his daughter's family. In the end, all charges were dropped, and he completed his term as vice president, though his name and political career were forever tarnished.[24] The historic home is now a beautiful B&B in this little gem of a town, rich with culture, delicious food, and open celebration of its many alleged haunted spots. The success of the Broadway production *Hamilton* shed a new spotlight on the duel and its surrounding history, and subsequently put the Aaron Burr House on the radar of Pennsylvanian paranormal enthusiasts, myself included.

In researching the building, I had heard claims of phantom voices throughout the building, objects moving on their own in the beautifully appointed guest rooms, and even the full-body apparition of a male figure in the stairwell. Some presumed it was Aaron Burr himself, but I am always cautious to attribute a definitive identity to any spirit, especially ahead of any personal experiences.

I booked a room with a friend for a weekday in November. Once we arrived and got settled into room 5, after a brief cup of coffee and a chat with the charming proprietor, we set up our equipment to begin. I set a REM-Pod and cat balls on the bed behind us as we filmed a brief introductory segment for an intended video. When my friend began discussing the differences in the legacies of Burr and Hamilton, I heard a faint male voice from our en suite bathroom to my left. I immediately checked, but it was empty and quiet. The building is a functioning hotel on a moderately busy street, so I wasn't quite ready to proclaim it "haunted" from one possible voice phenomenon, but we did decide to delay our dinner plans and launch into a brief Estes session first.

I sat in a chair in the corner of the room with a blindfold on and noise-canceling headphones hooked up to my SB-7. It was the typical rhythm of radio station clips blurring by my ears, though after a moment, I started to hear the same young male's voice come through repeatedly. Per standard Estes session methodology, I couldn't hear the questions being asked, but my oblivious responses, little by little, painted the portrait of a young male, possibly named "Philip," who may have been nineteen years old. I am cautious to not create too much of a constructed narrative around isolated Estes session remarks, preferring instead full phrases across many frequencies, so I mostly discounted the session.

However, interestingly, months later, while I was a guest on a paranormal podcast, the host mentioned he'd watched the video of the Aaron Burr House investigation I posted. He proceeded to tell me that the Estes session may have yielded more than I realized at the time; the site of the duel that killed Alexander Hamilton was indeed very near where Hamilton's son, Philip, died in a duel three years prior, at age nineteen. This information gave me chills. It also gave me mild guilt at not having connected the dots and acknowledging Philip's identity, if it was indeed his spirit attempting to communicate. It is, of course, only a name and a number linking the information, but I find it very interesting that such specific responses came through in a historically linked home.

Later that evening, I set up an abandonment session with a video camera and some cat balls on the bed in our guest room, and my friend and I sat in the common lounge area with another video camera, digital recorders, and a REM-Pod. We quickly discovered that the street noise often sounded much like the low voices of multiple people, thus likely disproving many of the claims of disembodied voices. At one point in the evening, the REM-Pod started beeping, and our momentary elation was dashed when we realized it was merely a low battery warning. I ran a video camera overnight in our room, but there was nothing paranormal of note on review. We packed up and headed our separate ways home, mildly disappointed by the quiet evening we'd had.

Gearing up for the Aaron Burr House, I had been so excited to investigate a location off the beaten path that I decided to film the evening in its entirety, aiming to produce my first full-length investigation video for social media. In the end, while the video was educational and enjoyable to make, it didn't include many paranormal experiences. That was when I first began to truly suspect the very act of filming more, with the intent to share, somehow blocked me from experiencing paranormal events in the first place. Sure, maybe the property is not haunted at all, or maybe I was distracted by equipment and camera angles and missed that true visceral connection. Or alternately, was I breaching some unspoken rule about paranormal investigating?

In all my years of consuming paranormal television and documentaries, there has never been one undeniable piece of evidence to truly prove anything supernatural. There are impressive and downright spooky captures, which have made me join in the hunt myself, but without being there at the time, how can any of us really trust what we see on TV or elsewhere? Though I'd previously filmed short clips or shared EVP clips online, in this bout I had focused much more on capturing visual paranormal experiments on film. Does having the intention to share the results of an investigation break some spiritual connection in that moment? Perhaps we, as a whole community, aren't meant to ever capture undeniable proof; perhaps it is a visceral thing – you must be there to inspire, witness, and appreciate the supernatural in the moment it happens. I suspect we are allowed snippets and hints of Other, but must lead ourselves the rest of the way, to Believing.

In the end, having a quiet investigation night is a positive experience, even if it is frustrating at the time. It makes evidence of other paranormal experiences you have in other locations that much more exciting; it's helpful to have a base-line to prove that you are a logical thinker and not automatically following the opinion of others, nor faking anything. Sometimes a spirit won't make themselves known to you. It's OK; honesty and logical reasoning must be paramount. The Aaron Burr House did not present itself to me as anything other than a beautifully tended B&B run by an extremely kind and courteous proprietor (who bakes homemade banana bread for guests each morning, by the way). I'd recommend it, just not for paranormal reasons.

On the other hand, sometimes there are those locations that won't easily give you that satisfying moment of evidence, but something in your bones just knows there is Other about it. This is how I feel about Bube's Brewery.

CHAPTER 20

BUBE'S BREWERY AND RESTAURANT

MOUNT JOY, PENNSYLVANIA

Bube's Brewery in Mount Joy, Pennsylvania, was founded in 1876 by a German immigrant named Alois Bube (yes, it's pronounced "BOO-beh"). German lager was becoming increasingly popular in the United States in the late 1800s, and Alois Bube had impeccable timing in opening his establishment. Having done well earning a respectable reputation both as a brewer and an employer, he expanded his business several times and built an adjoining hotel to accommodate overnight guests. They stored the beer in an underground cave beneath the property; the ambient cool temperature was perfect to keep the stored beer cold. Alois and his family lived on-site, and accounts often note that they were a happy, tight-knit family who were well liked in the community. Notably, one of Alois's granddaughters, Pauline, was schizophrenic, and instead of putting her into an institution where she may be the victim of dubious treatment programs, the family cared for her at home.

The brewery did very well, but unfortunately, Alois died suddenly in 1908, aged fifty-seven, at the height of his brewing career. The brewery did not do as well after his passing. The family had to sell the property in 1914 to a Swedish brewer named John Hallgren, who struggled to emulate Bube's success. A number of factors, including impending prohibition, forced Hallgren to sell the brewery. In 1920, Henry Engle, son-in-law of Alois Bube, took over the property; it was back in family hands. They operated the Central Hotel there until the late 1960s, and renovations began in 1968, continuing to this day.[25,26] The current owner purchased the property in 1982, and while he is not a member of the Bube family, his history of working at Bube's provided him with a deep affection for the location. Bube's earned a place on the National Register of Historic Places in 1973, as one of only hundreds of "lager era" breweries that still stands in almost completely intact condition.[27]

I first learned of Bube's when it was featured on a favorite paranormal TV show a little more than ten years ago. However, it wasn't until a few years ago, when an author friend featured a blurb about it in her atlas of haunted breweries, I realized how close the location was to me. I was quick to dive into the history of the brewery and its various paranormal claims. The brewery offers ghost tours daily, owing to the many claims of sightings of full-body apparitions on the property. The ghost of Alois's granddaughter Pauline is frequently claimed to be seen. Bartenders over the years claim to have seen a man walking through the front doors, and various disembodied voices (often in German) are heard throughout the property. Currently, Bube's seems to favor a local paranormal team, some of whom claim to regularly interact with a young girl on a particular side of the second-floor ballroom area.

The Catacombs restaurant is a wonderfully interesting location, set in the cave underneath Bube's Brewery. To get to your table in the rough-hewn stone chamber underneath the main building, a steep set of rickety stairs awaits you. Where once the brewers working for Alois Bube stored beer there to keep it cool, now there are flickering candles set into alcoves and fairy lights strung across the ceiling and along gigantic wooden kegs. It's a very special place to visit.

Shortly after realizing the restaurant's proximity to my home, I whisked my husband away for a dinner in the Catacombs. While he knew I was there to hopefully capture a spooky phenomenon over a glass of wine, he was fascinated to dine in such a unique setting. With an active stream running deep underneath the property, there's a certain constant damp quality to the air and certainly along the uneven stone floor beneath your feet. The proximity to running water makes me wonder if there is a connection to the property's paranormal claims and the theory of water energy.

ENERGY DRAIN AND WATER ENERGY

Another theory popular with paranormal investigators is that, presumably, a paranormal entity requires an energy source to manifest. Forming a visual bodily form, creating an audible sound, or making a detectable change in the electrical field requires some kind of energy. It has to come from somewhere. Without earthly bodies of their own, ghosts need an external energy source if they wish to interact. But where is that energy pulled from? What kind of energy can a spirit use? Does a visual manifestation require a more powerful energy draw than an auditory phenomenon? The rabbit hole goes deep on this one. Theories about the source of this borrowed energy abound.

One of the leading ideas is that ghosts can use energy from an actual battery, as simple as that. A diligent investigator will often charge up or replace batteries in all his or her pertinent equipment before an evening. Sometimes, they will find that only a few minutes into the investigation, the battery strength has fallen to zero. Flashlights may fail to work, or a device may just not turn on at all. Was it a nearby spirit using the energy, or just a mundane equipment malfunction? (Or nefarious dollar-store batteries, for that matter?)

Some investigators specifically bring devices to freely offer energy to a spirit. I myself have on occasion set out a plasma ball for a spirit to "use." Though I never witnessed the pink forks of electricity within the sphere react any differently, the ball has been present while I experienced some strange activity, so who is to say it wasn't effective? Some very well-funded televised teams even go so far as to use a Van de Graaff machine, a large and powerful electrostatic generator, to charge the environment for usage by spirits. Heat may also be a practical source; cold spots, possibly indicating a spirit has used the heat from the air to manifest, may be considered by some to be an energy drain.

Many investigators believe the natural environment plays a factor in a spirit's ability to access adequate energy, particularly in regard to water. Some of my most memorable paranormal experiences occurred in locations affected by the presence of water – at Gettysburg on a misty, rainy day, and at Fort Mifflin, where I was not only directly next to a major river, but underground in a damp tunnel, exploring the casemate cells, damp floors under the soles of my shoes.

In an industrial setting, when the kinetic energy of flowing water is captured and turned into electricity, it is called hydroelectric power, or hydropower. Hydropower is using water to power machinery or make electricity; perhaps in a haunted location this same premise is in play. Thunderstorms are commonly thought to aid manifestations, by both their impact on local electrical fields, and the influx of environmental kinetic energy of falling rain. Learning of a nearby flowing water in a stream or body of water is often cause for excitement amongst a group of investigators.

Taken a step further metaphysically, many cultures and spiritual belief systems consider water to be spiritually important as a clarifier, psychic amplifier, and as a record of history as it passes through its cycles in time. In conversation with others in the field, our comments inevitably spiraling more and more into abstract thoughts on the matter, a friend mentioned that perhaps it's simply just that humans throughout history have typically settled near water to maintain life. Perhaps proximity to water and increased activity simply means that life was more sustainable in that location, historically speaking. In Native American times up through Colonial settlers and even to the modern day, a geographic location near a water source would typically be richer in history of life and activity. If more people lived and died in a place, would there subsequently be more hauntings there? I find this to be a fascinating explanation as to why proximity to water may play a key component in paranormal activity.

Lastly, investigators themselves are sometimes considered to be sources of energy for spirits, like walking batteries. Some investigators believe strong emotion of the investigators themselves, say, fear energy, can be used by nearby spirits to manifest. I have experienced a sudden exhaustion after a great deal of activity on a night. Was a spirit using my energy to fuel their needs, thus depleting me? If other living humans can be draining, why not a ghost?

~

My favorite paranormal stories are ones in which the investigator references a phenomenon of battery drain or one of these energy-drain factors, followed soon after by an experience. When I am investigating or simply visiting a spooky location, and I notice a battery has died, or someone suddenly comments that they feel sleepy, I am instantly on alert, awaiting the manifestation that might follow. It's almost like a warning, anticipation of an incoming interesting moment. Spooky foreplay, if you will.

Since my first dining experience at Bube's, I've returned several times, sometimes as part of an investigation night, but others just for dinner or a nightcap at the bar. On subsequent visits I was able to tour the unusual guest rooms on the hotel side of the building. They are certainly a sight to see, each with a vibrantly decorated theme: some with suspended bedframes, ceiling mirrors, fake floor-to-ceiling trees and a jungle mural, and even dancing poles and disco balls. You will definitely have a memorable time visiting the guest rooms at the hotel, whether or not you see a ghost.

I have investigated overnight twice at Bube's, once at a public event, and once privately. Sometimes a haunted location will work in tandem with the same paranormal team repeatedly, allowing them a little more freedom and clearance in exchange for managing paranormal interest in the property and a share of any financial boon garnered. Suffice to say, sometimes that arrangement can create an uncomfortable scenario for investigators outside of that group.

On my most recent visit, I separated myself somewhat from the bulk of the group and hunkered down with a friend in what is called "the Priest's Room," off the bar area on the hotel side, which was once a gentlemen's club for gambling and drinking. We were seated at a table in this small room, while the rest of the group was outside the open doorway in the main bar area, running cameras, cat balls, and other various proximity equipment. My friend and I were sitting quietly as the other part of the group was asking questions for an EVP session despite a great deal of background noise from the still-open restaurant side. It would be nearly impossible to decipher a ghostly voice amongst the racket, but everyone was excited to get the investigation going as soon as possible.

As we sat at one end of a long table in the dark, we started to hear taps at the other end, seemingly in response to the rhythm of the questioning next door. Light filtered in through lace-curtained windows on two sides of us, but the corner from which the tapping sound came remained steadfastly dark. When another friend joined us at the table, we continued to hear the taps before a louder bang on the window behind her made us jump. We didn't draw attention to the sounds we were hearing, it felt like a fragile moment, and I didn't desire the rest of the group to crowd into the small room with us, potentially chasing it away. I had no other equipment with me – my gear bag was still upstairs, as we had been milling around the lobby, saying our hellos, and decided to just jump into a session. So with no better options and desiring something beyond my senses to attempt confirmation, I fired up an app on my phone. I don't generally believe digital apps like these to be worthwhile, but I will use them in a pinch or when activity is slow.

A few moments later, a member from the location's "home team" arrived unexpectedly and jumped into a lead role, boisterously asking questions for the ongoing EVP session. In my opinion, there wasn't nearly enough time between questions for any real response, and soon the volume in the room began to crescendo as the rest of the group began to join in. Someone would ask the spirit their age, another what they did in life, what does the afterlife look like, and even how they died. The questions came in a torrent; if there had been a spirit readying a response, he or she would be terribly confused and possibly offended by the quantity and types of queries. My friends and I shared incredulous glances, barely visible in the dim light, and just as my frustration level was rising with the haphazardness of it all, the app on my phone said, "GO AWAY," in tandem with a tap on the table. I laughed. Maybe Mr. Bube agreed with us. I don't put a lot of faith in digital apps, and call it an arrogant assumption, but we got the distinct impression that something in there with us was becoming just as irritable as we were. A grouchy ghost, that's a spirit I can connect with on occasion.

Later in the evening, I had finally gotten the chance to set up a REM-Pod in one of the upstairs rooms with a smaller group of friends, apart from the larger party that had assembled. After just a few minutes, we started having meaningfully timed responses on the REM-Pod – funnily enough, as we were playing around a bit with the dancer pole that had been mounted in the room. Yes, I'm serious, both about the pole's existence in this historic building, and the spirit response to our interacting with it. As my friend bent over, the REM-Pod went wild. (There's a case for paranormal libido.) Feeling we'd caught the spirit's attention with our mild antics, we decided to get serious and begin a short-burst EVP session. Just as we got set up, the entire party from the group dinner barreled into the room, cocktails in hand.

Minutes later, the moment descended into a scene from a nightclub. I looked around and felt so completely out of my investigating element and so disappointed that a real communication session had been interrupted. I was Party Pooper Incarnate, but there's a time and place for letting loose. I pride myself on being flexible, ready to go with the flow, but the spirit of the evening unfolding around me was not why I had left my family for a night. I appreciated my friend's invitation, and I love a good cocktail as much as the next mom, but realized I was done for the evening. I packed my gear, said my brief goodbyes, and started the drive home. I knew that I was officially closed off, and I made a call to remove myself from a situation that was no longer serving me or my desire to talk to ghosts.

A few months ago, on our way through town, my husband and I recently stopped by Bube's about an hour before it closed for the night. He's grown to love it there. Patrons were scant, and we enjoyed a quiet drink at the end of the near-empty bar. As we sat and sipped, I told him about my most recent experience investigating there, and now my husband is dead set on seeing this dancer pole with his own eyes. He says he wants to book one of the unique guest rooms for a night soon; maybe that will finally be my chance for a true EVP session. Overall, it's been fun to experience Bube's in so many different settings, even if some didn't match my intentions.

CHAPTER 21
THE HINSDALE HOUSE
HINSDALE, NEW YORK

One of the brightest spots in my paranormal adventures so far has been connecting with other women in the paranormal field. Inevitably and unfortunately, there are some negative aspects to jumping into any social media community, but as a nearly middle-aged mother, I've learned it's imperative to focus on the positives in any situation to wring the best out of life. This is often easier said than done, but worth the effort. Once I learned some tough lessons on finding my crowd, I was lucky enough to discover a circle of women in the field who truly support one another in their various successes. Some women in the paranormal write or make documentaries or run events or garner thousands upon thousands of social media followers, but however we embrace our spooky interests, what matters is the trust, respect, and friendship we build with one another.

On what we thought would be a sunny spring weekend in March of 2022, five women, myself included, whose writing was featured in the same women's paranormal journal, met in person at a haunted house in Hinsdale, New York, and promptly got stuck there in a blizzard. Luckily, we all fell instantly into a comfortable friendship together. It was a calculated gamble, meeting online friends for the first time, but even as it was in progress, we knew there was something special about that weekend. Getting snowed in by blizzard-like conditions during a paranormal investigation in upstate New York was a wildly unique experience.

There we were, five female paranormal investigators, camped out in the Hinsdale House, a two-level, weather-beaten farmhouse packed with wild ghostly claims, on the top of a snowy hill. The floors creak, and the stairwell is well worn. Metal screens cover each window to guard against the many curious visitors who stop by at any given hour, having heard the many ghost stories of what lies within. The modest building is buffered at the back by a dense patch of forest and a pond, each laden with their own ghostly claims. I was eager for my first crack at investigating Hinsdale for myself.

I sometimes go into haunted locations intentionally igno-rant of the history and conduct my historical research after-ward, so that I may have a clean slate from which to interpret my experiences. I dislike being flat-out told what or espe-cially *who* to expect; I find it clouds objectiveness when inves-tigators go in expecting certain types of activity. It isn't always feasible to go in blind, but I make the attempt to do so. I had seen the Hinsdale House featured elsewhere and knew it was often surrounded by claims of demonic activity and "dark energy." However, I also know that the paranormal community all too often falls into the pattern of patently accepting what is told, and the spookier and more fantasti-cal, the better. It's fun for Halloween, but inappropriate in cases of real hauntings. Exaggerated information in the para-normal field isn't new, but it never becomes less tiresomeIn the end, pre-categorizing activity as dark and malicious is unfair to any actual spirits lingering on-site, wishing to communicate.

I've learned that despite popular accounts of Hinsdale's history, the facts behind the location's past may not exactly coincide, for whatever reason. In a nutshell, what has been documented is the Hinsdale House was built in the mid-1800s by David Everts. In 1858, it was sold to a man named Alfred Burton, and then in 1861 to Michael McMahon, for whom the road out front is named. In the 1970s, there was a series of unexplainable events at the house, which terribly frightened the residents at the time, the Dandy family.[28] Clara Miller, who was married to Phillip Dandy, wrote a book, *Echoes of a Haunting*, to relay the eerie experiences she had while living at the Hinsdale House with her family. The book tells of hearing a choir singing in the woods behind the home, a dark-haired woman walking through the house or peering in the windows, and even items flying off shelves in the middle of the night.[29] These events would indeed be frightening to experience in your own home, but none sounds particularly demonic in nature. There are some legends of murder on the property that are currently unproven, and a priest came to cleanse the house for the Dandy family. All told, in the end, our paranormal experiences that cold night were indeed interesting, though not nearly as "dark" as we were assured they would be.

Within ten minutes of our private time on the property, one of my friends launched into an impassioned speech on a gripe we all shared. As she concluded her speech, a picture frame in the bathroom behind her promptly came flying off the wall and crashed into the sink, hitting the light switch into the off position on the way down. We were all stunned. We were still setting up as she spoke, so we did not catch video evidence, but we all saw it with our own eyes. My friend had not been stomping her feet or gesticulating anywhere near the wall on which the picture was hung. We rehung it on the protruding nail and slammed into the back of the wall, but the frame stayed put. I have never seen an object move in front of my eyes on an investigation before; it really started our night's adventures with a bang, so to speak. We wondered what was in store for the night ahead.

POLTERGEIST ACTIVITY

The movement of items by an unseen hand, like falling objects or banging doors, is often referred to as "poltergeist activity." In a recent (and hilariously frenzied) online poll I posted, and in subsequent conversations with over twenty of my paranormal friends, there was one thing we all agreed upon: this topic is a mind-bender. It seems that in the paranormal community of the moment, the current definition of the term has a lot of nuances. The input I received was progressively more animated, arguing various points (sometimes with themselves) about the concept. While the term "poltergeist" is literally defined as "noisy or knocking spirit" from its German linguistic origin, its colloquial usage isn't so straightforward. I blame Hollywood, as much as I adore Craig T. Nelson.

While "poltergeist" is commonly used as an accepted term for a theoretical entity that can move objects, in the paranormal community, "poltergeist activity" can actually refer to the movement itself without especially defining the spirit in question. For example, many of the investigators I polled have said or *would* say, "The spirit showed signs of poltergeist activity," without classifying the spirit in question as a "poltergeist." As someone who enjoys organization and the tidiness of clearly defined terms (a rarity in this field), I can't help but crave more information. For those who believe in poltergeists as a separate classification of entities, if they can move physical objects on our plane, are they therefore stronger than the "average" ghost? Is that all that differentiates them? I think I must submit to ambiguity in this case, as much as it irks me.

There is a popular complementary theory regarding poltergeist activity in a haunting: it can actually be unconsciously caused by living persons nearby; strong emotion or high stress can physically affect the environment. Poltergeist activity is often thought to be linked to pubescent girls in particular. This is not to say they have mystical powers of some kind and can manipulate the environment at will, but that their rapidly changing physiology and subsequent stress, both physical and emotional, can somehow affect their surroundings. From this perspective, we are contributing to the very haunting we are researching: a rabbit hole indeed.

I am not sure where I stand on the definition of "poltergeist activity," its causes, or even its existence, but until my time at Hinsdale, I had never seen an object move during an investigation. It was particularly unusual that it happened to occur right after a moment of raw frustration, not to mention at a time when none of us was filming, which aligns with my previously held belief that recording devices somehow affect activity. Then again, perhaps the spirits simply agreed with my friend and were keen to let us know. Or maybe they just don't like that picture.

J ust a little later that evening, once we were finally set up (more speedily than usual – after the frame flew off the wall, we were anxious to start recording) and ready to begin some dedicated sessions, suddenly a few of us experienced battery drain on our equipment. A fully charged temperature fluctuation gauge was dead in minutes. I'd hoped for a manifestation to follow shortly after that, possibly the spirits draining energy for something tangible, but nothing further occurred in that moment. I had also wondered if the falling snow outside would lend itself in the way of water energy to spirit activity on-site, and looked forward to the night's possibilities. There were a lot of interesting factors in play.

We replaced batteries once again and sat down to introduce ourselves to the house and get comfortable in the space. But as friends do, as we were all just sitting down together for the first time, we couldn't help but launch into exuberant conversation, getting to know each other and finding that we were all hilarious, in our own opinions. It was lovely to see the need for female comradery reflected back at me from the wonderfully weird women surrounding me. I enjoyed the animated conversation while I kept an ear and eye out for anything ghostly. After a while, mid-conversation, I suddenly noticed an extra female voice joining the din. I said nothing to the group the first time I heard it, mentally dismissing it and returning to the conversation. Upon repeatedly hearing the same faint high-pitched feminine voice, just a few syllables at a time, coming from upstairs, I grabbed everyone's attention so they could listen too. I waited with bated breath, ears toward the stairwell, and when I heard the soft voice again, I bounded up the travel-beaten stairs to check it out.

Finding nothing, we all paused in the room, stock-still,

waiting. We all heard thumping and movement coming from the vicinity of the crawlspace across from the stairs, above the kitchen. I straddled the threshold of the small bedroom at the top of the stairs, avoiding looking at the creepy porcelain doll staring up at me from its ramshackle stroller. We were starting to wonder aloud if perhaps animals were getting into the crawlspace and making noise. Just then, I heard a sudden inhale of breath just inches from my left ear, as if someone were about to scream. No shout came, but I was rattled, and I whirled back and raised my flashlight toward the creepy room, expecting the face of a Babadook to materialize. My flashlight beam trembled slightly as my heart rate came back down to a reasonable pace, but nothing else happened.

Frustratingly, no one but myself heard either the feminine voice or the sharp inhale, so I had to chalk both up to a personal experience. I had a flash of remembering my night at the Shanley Hotel, in which I seemed to be singled out for spooky experiences for the evening, and hoped instead we'd soon all share experiences together. I didn't want to appear like I was calling "ghost" every ten minutes in front of people I had just met. After a few more minutes of quiet stillness, we ventured back downstairs to the living room and proceeded to run Estes sessions in turns.

Towards the end of our multiple mostly quiet sessions, one of the investigators noticed through the mesh-covered hole in the ceiling that peeks into the upstairs bedroom that the house's motion-sensor light had come on. Minutes later, we heard a loud thump, as if the bedframe had shifted. We crept up the stairs to move our investigation, following the activity. Turning all the lights off, we stood still, willing something to happen. Suddenly, all five of us heard the familiar *clack, clack, clack* sound of animal nails on the kitchen floor just at the bottom of the stairs, followed by what sounded like the tags on a dog collar jingling. It was so clear and recognizable that I thought a neighbor's pet had somehow broken into the house to take shelter from the snowstorm raging outside. I was closest to the top of the stairs, and I suddenly peeked out, hoping to glimpse an animal, real or ghostly, but saw nothing.

I found later, upon review of the camera I had running in the upstairs bedroom during our Estes sessions, that the motion light was likely triggered due to mice dashing through the room. It's interesting that we had been drawn as a group back upstairs, only to hear sounds downstairs. We never found any plausible reason to explain away the unmistakable animal sounds that came from the kitchen, but I was pleased that we all heard it, unanimously.

After the "ghost dog," another first for me on an investigation, we relocated back down to the living room, and the rest of the night was well spent getting to know each other, eating way too many snacks, sharing stories, and laughing. The previously isolated, stay-at-home-mom part of myself was overjoyed. Whether the spirits respected our female retreat energy and left us to enjoy it, or they were done with us for the evening, (or they don't exist), we didn't get much more in the way of paranormal activity that night.

Once, in the middle of the night, when getting up to use the restroom, I quickly checked the footage from the camera I'd set running in the kitchen, but saw nothing unusual. Though the friend sleeping on the couch said she heard footsteps next to her, I didn't catch it on the camera. That night as we slept, the blizzard intensified to its full force.

The next day we awoke, groggy but enthusiastic about our previous evening. We were in the unique situation of being snowed into a haunted house, forced to wait a few hours to depart until the snow died down enough to travel safely to our second night's location. We wrapped our sleeping bags around our shoulders and congregated in the living room to slowly wake up in mind and body. My friend and I shuffled into the kitchen area to gingerly prepare cups of coffee. We watched the snowflakes drift lazily down outside, and I felt such peace sitting in that weird and supposedly haunted house. The weekend of female collaboration was a balm to my soul and further proof that somewhere along the way I had made the right decision in pursuing a place in this field.

Eventually, between becoming stir-crazy and getting anxious to head to our second night of the double-header weekend of investigating, we swapped pajamas for clothes, packed our gear, and headed out, thanking the spirits as we left. (That's just good manners, really.) It was still snowing in upstate New York, and my friend was kind enough to take the task of driving while I white-knuckled it in the passenger seat. Ghost hunts, yes. Driving in snow? No.

As we headed toward a restaurant halfway between Hinsdale and our next haunted stop, I pondered how our time the previous evening did not match what we had been told to expect (i.e., a "dark and evil demonic presence"). We didn't see any actual corporeal entities, nor did we feel threatened at any point, though we did sense that something had made a feeble attempt to communicate. I mulled over the idea that perhaps what haunts Hinsdale, if anything, is an egregore.

EGREGORES

Without doubt, the topic of egregores is one of the wilder concepts I've sat with since entering the paranormal field, but also one of the most fascinating. I personally have found the theory to be a potential fit for a few of my experiences, including my time at Hinsdale.

An egregore, alternately spelled aggregore, and sometimes

called a thoughtform, is an entity inadvertently manufactured by the collective energies and intentions of many people in or about one location. In simpler terms, think of it as all of our collective thoughts and energies layering one on top of another over time. These layers may somehow unconsciously create a large, immaterial force that projects back to us from the environment around us. If enough people are thinking the same thoughts and projecting the same energy out and toward one specific location, perhaps an amalgamation of that energy could form and hold that space, enough so that others could experience it.

It's a wild theory, one that heavily relies on the idea of collective unconscious and energy. It's an odd concept, but one you can see at work in times of the year when the same ideas or emotions are all directed toward a similar thought. For example, think of Christmastime, when everyone seems just a little bit cheerier, December days holding a little more magic than the rest of the year. The general joyful feeling in the air is a collection of collective excitement and holiday merriment. Many people are focusing on the same kinds of thoughts and emotions at the same time, contributing to the "most wonderful time of the year."

An egregore, on the paranormal spectrum, may form over a very long period of time, with a lot of people thinking along the same lines over and over. If every investigator coming into a haunted place is walking in expecting a child spirit with brown hair, after long enough, perhaps a small, brunette spirit will, in fact, materialize.

Sometimes the term "tulpa" or "servitor" will be casually used interchangeably for the term "egregore," but according to experts, a tulpa is thought generally to be an entity *purposefully* conjured by one individual, usually with religious origins. The origins of the tulpa concept date back to the early 1900s, with an occultist named Alexandra David Neel supposedly conjuring a tulpa of a monk in Tibet.

There are several pseudoscientific studies on the subject of egregores, most notably, the Philip Experiment. In 1972, a group of parapsychologists in Toronto attempted to create a fictional character through purposeful, concentrated, directed thought, and then communicate with him through séance. They named their fictional character Philip Aylesford and created an entire imaginary backstory for him. He was born in 1624 in England, had an early military career, and even had a melodramatic love life, eventually dying by suicide at the age of thirty. After weeks of intense directed thought toward "Philip," the group was seated around a table with initial séances yielding no contact. When one of the group leaders dimmed the lights, participants claimed to begin feeling a presence, and heard rapping sounds that matched responses to questions about Philip's life. The séance reached its zenith of activity when at one point the table tilted on a single leg, and at other times moved across the room without human contact. As one can imagine, the "study" was met with a great deal of criticism, both then and now, but it remains an interesting case and point of study for those interested in the theory.[30,31,32]

As a facetious aside, as an avid fiction reader, I've wondered if there are accidental egregores of some of the steamier romantic hero characters from some of my favorite books wandering around somewhere. With millions of copies sold, extensively detailed backgrounds written, and enough fan art to fill an entire corner of the internet, if egregores exist, that has to have fueled at least one. If you know where he is, let me know, please.

But in all seriousness, the idea of an egregore repeatedly catches my attention. We have all experienced moments in which a group gets swept up in a strong emotion or singular cause. Is it really so strange to think that this energy lingers?

~

Hinsdale has garnered the attention of many investigators over a long period of time, likely coming in with certain expectations based on what they've been told. I'd imagine it has been difficult for investigators booking the property to arrive without the bias of expecting negative activity; maybe they're bringing it along with them. Maybe they're making their own ghosts.

CHAPTER 22
WILDWOOD SANITARIUM
SALAMANCA, NEW YORK

The Wildwood Sanitarium is an odd little building squatting on a quiet street in a small neighborhood in western New York State. The home has a somewhat chaotic atmosphere, with its unusual internal architecture, relics of its various past identities as a hospital and separate apartments. I most definitely (and embarrassingly) got lost more than once during our overnight stay, on livestreamed video, no less, trying to find my way back from the third floor via various confusing stairwells that did not end where I expected them to. The building itself is not the typical sprawling behemoth we expect to pull up to when we hear the word "sanitarium"; rather, it is an average-sized stone house with a wraparound porch and turret in the front. The building owner obviously cares a great deal about the location and seems to be forever making repairs to maintain the building's integrity.

When we arrived after a slippery, snowy drive across town, she was kind enough to give us a thorough history tour of the building and a recap of its ghostly claims. Particular hotspots of interest included an upstairs séance room, complete with a pendulum suspended over a small sand basin. Another invariably creepy spot in the sanitarium is the basement, the original location of the battery baths used as treatment for patients, and an embalming table, not original to the location but creepy nonetheless.

The sanitarium was at one point a center for holistic medicine for noncontagious diseases and addiction in the small town of Salamanca. It was a wellness center for the affluent, not having ever been a large hospital with many beds and state funding, which is the usual "haunted sanitarium" backstory. It was run by two young doctors, Dr. John Henderson and Dr. Carroll W. Perry. According to the owner, in 1923, they were forced to begin taking in tuberculosis patients. When the sanitarium closed down in the mid-1940s, the property was almost immediately divided into apartments, hence the present-day internal architecture, with its unexpected stairwells and doorframes. It moved into the hands of the current owner in 2017, and she began having paranormal experiences there soon after. The site is very popular for bookings with paranormal groups and has been featured on various paranormal television shows over the years. Most notably, a mirror suddenly fell off the wall while filming one of these programs, a moment memorialized in the house.

We began our investigation of the property with taking photos as we walked back through after the tour, and sat for a few periods of quiet listening sessions without much activity. Truth be told, we couldn't resist some wonderfully macabre photos on the embalming table and in the old battery baths. We dove into conversations about the paranormal, our various experiences so far, and what we hoped to accomplish in future. Through these conversations, I realized I wanted to write about my paranormal journey. I'd always loved writing, and it clicked for me that I wanted to document the strange things I'd experienced, how I'd changed since my first investigation, and how I make time for it, even as a busy mom.

After a paranormal "game" led by a friend, in which I miserably (but hopefully comically) failed in navigating the house on my own to find a hidden Post-it note, we were ready to get back to reaching out more seriously. We headed upstairs to the séance room for an EVP session, and while we heard a few bumps and creaks coming from the back upstairs kitchen area, no responses of true consequence came through. We moved on to an upstairs bedroom, all of us starting to succumb to the late hour despite the intake of our many energy drinks. We watched the snow continue to fall around our cars parked out front, and, not experiencing much more, decided to wrap up. We stepped carefully around the many creepy dolls lining the hallways and fell into various beds on various floors of the house. I wrapped myself deeply into my sleeping bag, trying to keep my eyes open long enough to see a shadow figure move across the doorway of the next room, but I saw nothing unusual before sleep claimed me.

In the morning, we clumsily, groggily made our way out of our beds and began packing gear. I was thankful for my snow boots as I trudged through the bitterly cold morning, packing my friend's car for the long drive home to Pennsylvania. As I hugged my new ghoul-friends goodbye, I felt immensely grateful for such a special sisterhood weekend with its spooky moments, but mostly for the female friendship and laughter. And the onion dip.

PART THREE

MACABRE EXPLORATIONS

CHAPTER 23
"SORRY, OCCUPIED!"

When I was in high school, aged seventeen or so, I had a strange occurrence at the least spooky location I could ever think of, even if I tried – the women's room of a Red Lobster restaurant. Yes, I'm serious. I was out to an early dinner with my parents one random day, enjoying the famous epic cheese biscuits, when I needed to excuse myself to the ladies' room. The bathroom was oddly decorated – map-print wallpaper covered every wall, including the sloping ceiling of the room, giving the room a claustrophobic feel. It had three stalls and a typical sink and mirror area next to the door, which closed on a strike plate so the door would never slam shut.

I went into the farthest stall, with the wall to my immediate right. As I was finishing up, there was suddenly a very loud slam on my stall door. I let out a tiny yelp, having been startled so suddenly – I hadn't heard anyone come in. I called out, "Just a minute, please!" as I got myself together. Mere moments later, there was another loud banging on the door; I could see the door literally slamming against the hinges. I called out again, less politely this time, "I said just a minute!" At this time, I peeked under the wall to my left, and seeing no occupants in the other two stalls, I said as much to the mysterious impatient woman waiting outside my stall. I didn't notice any feet beyond my door, but the stall was rather small, the door right up to my knees, and I wasn't in the spooky mindset at the time to check if this angry person did, in fact, have legs. I heard nothing and presumed the woman had taken my annoyed tone and was calmly waiting for what was apparently her favorite toilet stall. As I stood to zip my jeans, again there was a loud BANG on the door. At this point, I didn't even say anything, as I was ready to whip the door open, almost as the banging was still occurring.

No one.

There was no irate, full-bladdered woman ready to barge past me into my stall like I expected, no one in the other two still-empty stalls, and the bathroom door, a good six feet away, wasn't slowly closing on its mechanical stopper. As my brain struggled to comprehend what was happening, I realized that my hands were as cold as ice. Indeed, my nose was cold as well. I glanced at my reflection in the mirror across from my stall for a moment before deciding to get the hell out of that room. (No, I did not wash my hands.)

The restaurant was free-standing in a strip mall parking lot, and the kitchen was not adjacent to the bathroom, if you're thinking along the same lines I did – that something had fallen into the wall from the other side, or something similar that would have caused the cacophony. That also wouldn't explain the individual door rattling on its hinges in front of my eyes and its sudden cessation when I pulled the door open. Suffice to say, through the years, I have vaguely chalked up that odd (and slightly comical, retrospectively) incident to perhaps a haunting of the land and not necessarily a seafood-related

MAKING FRIENDS WITH GHOSTS

spirit. (An angry lobster seeking vengeance?) Northern New Jersey has a past rich in Native American history, and while far too many haunted tales seem to casually loop in "Native American burial grounds," it is legitimately fair and right to never fully discount that historical tapestry and its possible effect on modern buildings and unexplainable activity therein.

I have always loved a spooky experience even, or *especially*, where and when I don't expect it.

CHAPTER 24
HAUNTED CAFÉS ARE MY FAVORITE

As a paranormal investigator, the constant pull of wanting to explore the spooky underbelly of everything has quite the draw. In my history class in high school, my mind always inevitably wandered as I read page after page of dates and names of faceless individuals from the past. Nothing I read of impactful moments in history had meaning beyond a decent grade on the next exam. An unexpected facet of being in the paranormal field is seeing historically significant locations with fresh eyes. If potential hauntings or macabre tidbits are present in the history of a tavern or inn of note, my attention is perked up, and I am focused, even if it's not in a full, elaborate investigation setting.

Sometimes, to my dismay, I am physically unable to schedule time away for a full investigation weekend at a haunted location. The responsibilities of my role as "mom" dictate that I am home more often than not, and having no nanny or village of support dramatically reduces my free time for spooky endeavors. So, while I try to book as many overnights as I can, more commonly, I am instead going on day trips to interesting macabre locations while my children are in school, or toting them along with me.

I will go out of my way to dine at a haunted restaurant, just to have a glance around. I'll drag my husband (the last straw of his patience trailing behind him) across a city for a pint at a haunted bar with a grisly past. When we check into hotels, you can be sure I've already searched online for the most haunted hotel in the area and requested the most haunted room. If there's a park or a shop with a creepy story within reasonable driving distance, it finds its way onto my schedule. Even if I am not formally investigating with my equipment case handy, I will attempt to visit interesting places if they hold a whisper of ghosts. The following are accounts of a few of my "macabre explorations," as I have come to call them, each with varying levels of spooky experiences, but each with interesting and sometimes dark history. Each visit is a thread woven into the tapestry of my paranormal adventure.

CHAPTER 25

MCCOOLE'S AT THE RED LION INN

QUAKERTOWN, PENNSYLVANIA

T he Red Lion Inn had been on my radar for years until I was finally able to make the time to visit early one spring. Situated off the main road between my home and my brother's house in the next county over, I have passed it countless times and longed to go. My interest was keen, especially knowing it was a haunted favorite amongst some Philadelphia-based paranormal celebrities.

The inn was originally owned by Walter McCoole and opened in the late 1740s to the general shock of the local neighborhood mostly comprised of Quakers, who abstain from alcohol. Over time, however, the proprietors of the inn and the community developed an amiable relationship, and the tavern did well. In 1793, its name was changed to Enoch's Tavern, and it was used as the meeting place for the organizers of Fries Rebellion, led by German-Pennsylvanian John Fries.[33] He and his followers were outraged over new taxes that disproportionately targeted their ethnic group. Fries led a protest, after which Alexander Hamilton declared Fries and his group to be traitors under legislation criminalizing dissent, and charged them with treason. They were found guilty in court and were to be hanged at a location near the Red Lion Inn. President John Adams granted amnesty to John Fries and his brethren just hours before their scheduled executions in May 1800.[34]

In addition to its significance in the period after the Revolutionary War, in later years, McCoole's was part of the Underground Railroad. Some of the tunnels that connect the inn to the refugee tunnel system running under Quakertown supposedly still exist underneath the inn today. McCoole's staff and customers alike claim to see clear apparitions of ladies, men and children. In the women's room in particular, it is not uncommon to see a woman dressed in Victorian-style clothing in the mirror behind you. With this hefty historic past and the many visual paranormal claims on the property, I knew I needed to finally prioritize a visit.

It was interesting to see the location for myself after hearing so much about it. I sat at a table just outside the main dining area, within view of the original fireplace and the adjacent bar area. I had lunch with my friend, who was at the time my paranormal teammate, and we ran equipment as we ate a light lunch with our daughters, keeping one ear on our surroundings and eyes peeled for anything unusual.

The tale of the Victorian-styled woman seen in the mirror of the women's room has always especially piqued my interest. I made a point to go in and snap a few shots in the mirror, but unfortunately, I was alone in the resulting photos. I did get a slightly uncomfortable feeling in there alone, which isn't always the case on brief daytime visits. I'd be very curious to head back and sit in the quiet dark, to see what secrets unfolded around me. I would also hope for access to the basement area, where the claims of disembodied voices reign.

My friend and I finished our meal, enjoyed a cup of coffee, remarking that the equipment had been mostly quiet. Oddly enough, the *Ovilus* said "jackets" as we dressed our daughters in their coats, but that was the only suspicious moment of note. We went our separate ways, but I made a mental note to look into overnight bookings. I imagine the energy is palpably different at night with all the patrons gone, but I probably wouldn't rush back to this spot above others on my list for its ghostly activity level, based on my daytime foray here, though the coffee was good.

CHAPTER 26
THE SEVEN STARS INN
PHOENIXVILLE, PENNSYLVANIA

O ne of my favorite supposedly haunted restaurants near my home is the Seven Stars Inn in Phoenixville, Pennsylvania. It boasts cozy tables for romantic dinners, with a subtly spooky atmosphere as well. The haunted history of the restaurant is a little murky; in the mid-1700s to early 1800s, multiple pubs and inns in the area were named "Seven Stars Inn," as innkeepers at the time generally took the name of their establishment with them if they moved around a lot, which they did.[35]

There's a sad tale often wrongly attributed to this particular restaurant, though the story itself is indeed true. In 1837, the elderly wife of a Seven Stars Inn proprietor, Rachel Parker, was murdered, and the culprit was never discovered nor brought to justice. Reports of an apparition of an old woman on the stairs of the restaurant are prevalent, though the actual establishment where she was murdered is about a mile away.

I have a few theories as to these claims of this female spirit. Perhaps people hear the story and their experiences are naturally skewed to see an old woman, or perhaps it is that of another nameless woman yet to be identified. Maybe it really is Rachel, lingering in a location not too far from her original home, awaiting justice for her murder. Then again, do we as paranormal investigators hear "murder" and just assume that a ghost remains? Sometimes I'm frustrated that I haven't had a particular experience myself, simply because I want to have my own unsullied information about a claim. The story of Rachel Parker is one of those tales that keeps me returning to the location.

The inn is also said to be haunted by two male spirits, one in the upstairs dining room, and the other a young boy in riding clothes. I love nothing better than when haunting claims include full-body apparitions, so when my husband and I manage to get a babysitter, we often opt to head to the Seven Stars. Sadly, I have yet to experience anything paranormal on my visits to the spot. However, I have often enjoyed a few martinis on each of my visits, so perhaps I did and didn't realize it at the time.

CHAPTER 27

BRINTON LODGE

DOUGLASSVILLE, PENNSYLVANIA

I'd never deny that I don't mind when a haunted location also happens to serve up tasty adult beverages. If I'm not formally investigating, I see nothing wrong with enjoying a cocktail while I casually look around for spooky stuff. I recently dragged my husband and children out to visit Brinton Lodge, a lovely historic home that shares its site with a brewing company known for their IPAs.

The original structure at Brinton Lodge was at first a small farmhouse built in the early 1700s by the Millard family, one of the earliest families to purchase land from William Penn, the founder of the state. The farmhouse was eventually owned by the Kirlin family until the early 1900s, when it was then purchased by the Wittmans, who built their mansion around the original farmhouse. Subsequently, the building has a layered quality to it, both spiritually and architecturally, with unexpected thresholds dotting the path through the house, and internal windows looking into adjacent rooms.

During Prohibition, the lodge came under the ownership of hotelier Caleb Brinton, who opened it as an exclusive gentlemen's club and, presumably, a speakeasy. More recently, the lodge operated as "Covatta's Brinton Lodge Restaurant" for many years before transforming into the current hotspot – Hidden River Brewing Company, run by two brothers-in-law.[36] The brewery has a great vibe for weekend drinks, with outdoor seating and a grassy lawn along the Schuylkill Canal. But despite the quality of the drinks at hand, it was, of course, the spirits of the lodge I wished to encounter first and foremost.

Supposedly, among the ghostly residents are former owners Katharine Wittman and Caleb Brinton, who have each been sighted on the stairwell, the latter of whom tips his derby hat to women. The lodge claims to have a rather flirtatious spirit whom they've named "Dapper Dan," who apparently likes to blow in the ears of female guests, as well as pinch their rears. These saucy speakeasy-era ghost claims always seem to be a little naughty.

At the time, when I asked at the bar if I would be able to book an overnight investigation, businesses were still finding their way in the newly post-Covid world, and they weren't admitting paranormal investigators in, though signs on the bar proclaimed that the building was, in fact, one of the "10 most haunted houses in Pennsylvania." So a peek around the public spaces of the building had to suffice. Even that small taste, however, hit alarms on my spooky radar, to be sure.

I briefly stepped away from my family, who were preoccupied with finding kid-friendly beverages, and took myself on a leisurely tour of the first floor of the lodge. As I was filming some short video clips of the main stairwell and just getting the first sensations of a creepy Otherworldly vibe, perhaps recognizing my devoted attention, I unintentionally picked up a tour guide who I think was either trying to frighten or flirt with me, or both, by telling me about the ghost stories of the room we were standing in. His blank stare in response to my follow-up questions told me he wasn't quite prepared for the level of detail I sought about the ghosts. When my husband came to find me, my tour guide abruptly excused himself, and I was left wondering if a portion of the creepy vibe I had started to sense was in fact ghostly, or simply... human.

I continued my stroll through the rooms, soaking in views of all the old photographs and wishing I could run up the stairs for a peek. A separate bartender reiterated, at my questioning, that the second story and beyond are off-limits unless on a ghost tour or private investigation, which they weren't scheduling at the time. But to be honest, even with the giggles of children and general merriment taking place just outside on the lawn next to the river, I felt the pull of that good old creepy vibe as soon as I saw the main staircase. As of the time of writing, they have restarted their guided ghost tour program. I sense a spooky night out approaching.

CHAPTER 28

THE HOTEL BETHLEHEM
BETHLEHEM, PENNSYLVANIA

I was lucky enough to spend a night at the Hotel Bethlehem in Bethlehem, Pennsylvania, last fall. This mom very much needed a night away, and I'm always thrilled to loop in something haunted and macabre, even on a romantic night away with my husband. This beautiful building has all manner of accolades for its hospitality and historical significance in the area and a proud celebration of its hauntings – just the ticket.

The Hotel Bethlehem is a beautiful, towering 125-room hotel on the list of Historic Hotels of America and is on the National Register of Historic Places. Bethlehem itself is rich in Moravian history, and the town has grown into a boutique destination, with many shops, cafés, and restaurants, and has a particularly busy Christmas season, with its festive name and religious roots.

The hotel sits on the same plot of land that the first house in Bethlehem was built, the Moravian missionaries' log house, which unfortunately was torn down to make room for more modern structures. The site of the hotel was originally a general store in 1794, when the town was frequented by General George Washington. In 1822, the building was converted into the Golden Eagle Hotel and enjoyed nearly one hundred years of thriving business in the quaint Moravian town. However, that building was demolished in 1920 to be replaced with a more fireproof structure, now called the Hotel Bethlehem, backed with major funding from steel giant Charles Schwab and others from Bethlehem Steel.

Despite the fireproof improvements seventy years prior, one fateful day years later, on January 29, 1989, a fire in a guest room got out of control, and four people died on the fifth floor.[37] In the 1990s, the hotel's funding declined, but luckily, a group of local investors banded together and purchased the defunct Hotel Bethlehem, who have since restored it to its former splendor, to my delight.

The hotel is straightforward about what they call their "friendly spirits," and they claim to have identified at least three of them by name. According to the hotel, the most frequent sighting is of Mary Augusta "May" Yohé, a musical theater actress who was literally born in the Golden Eagle Hotel in April 1866. She was a performer all her life, singing and dancing for guests at the hotel as a child going on to become a traveling performer in the early 1900s. Guests claim to see her apparition in the third-floor lobby and in the exercise area.

Another ghost said to haunt Hotel Bethlehem is Francis "Daddy" Thomas, a deliveryman with a cheerful demeanor who has been sighted in the hotel's boiler room. The third "identified" spirit is actually a couple, Mr. and Mrs. Brong, who were semipermanent residents of the Golden Eagle Hotel before its demolition, and who were asked to leave the premises when hotel guests constantly complained that Mrs. Brong always had bare feet. Notably, her apparition is said to always be seen with bare feet; this is presumably how they identified her. She is said to appear in the hotel's restaurant to irritate hotel staff as an act of minor vengeance.

The fourth and most mysterious ghost was the spirit of the most interest to me on this trip, due simply to its apparent elusiveness. This unidentified spirit of room 932 is claimed to be the culprit behind shadow figures seen in the room, moved personal belongings, papers and books seen standing on end, and faces in the mirror. I had asked for room 932 at booking, but sadly it had been taken; we were arriving during a boisterous street festival in town. We were, however, only a few doors down the hallway from room 932. I quietly crept down the hallway to attempt to reach out psychically and see if I got a sense of anything. But I have to say, I think most if not all long, empty hotel hallways have that classic horror-movie creep factor.

So although we weren't in the "hotspot" room, I was happy to be nearby, at least. This wasn't specifically an investigation weekend – and good thing too, that festival was very energetic – but I wanted to at least try to capture something. Luckily, my husband is a good sport. After we checked in, I set up an abandonment session in the room, with my video camera facing some cat balls and a K2 meter on the writing desk. I was hoping to capture any of the claims of movement or EVP in our room while we went out to enjoy the festival and when we went out to dinner at a local speakeasy-themed restaurant later.

Unfortunately, most of the video footage from before bedtime had to be tossed; the live music from the harvest festival outside was easily audible through the window, so any vocal phenomena were corrupted. All I managed to capture during the day were the puzzled expressions of two hotel employees as they delivered the charcuterie board I had ordered as a surprise for my husband, and then spotted the camera. Who knows what they thought I had planned for the evening? It must have seemed quite scandalous. Or just weird.

After dinner, before we went to bed that evening, I decided to leave the video camera running for a few hours. Presumably I'd awaken out of a doze at some point in the night (a usual habit) and turn it off, or the memory card would be exhausted and it would turn itself off at some point. I set it facing toward my feet with the K2 in the foreground and cat balls around the room, to my skeptic husband's mirth. As it happens, around 3 a.m. he and I were both awoken by the entire room flashing with lights from the K2 and all of the cat balls simultaneously flashing. The room was bathed in a frenzy of blue and red lights flashing in chaotic succession – not the most peaceful way to be abruptly awakened.

As I groggily came to conscious thought from the light show, I thought perhaps the police had come for an altercation in the late-night remnants of the festival outside, but then remembered we were up on the ninth floor. When I rubbed my eyes and saw the cat balls and K2 meter flashing in opposite areas of the room, I had instant chills. Even my husband was shocked and a little creeped out. The room we were staying in wasn't reportedly the most haunted room, but the room in question was only a few doors down the hallway, after all, and earlier in the day, I had vocally invited the spirit to come say hello to us. I clumsily scrambled over to my video camera to make sure I was capturing everything, but the camera had turned itself off by then. "Of course it did," I wryly thought to myself. As I fumbled with sleep-stiff fingers to get it turned back on, the lights stopped. By the time I was ready to record again, the room was still and dark once more.

It was almost as if the spirit activity knew I'd been set up to catch it, and ceased the moment I would be able to do so. This type of start-and-stop activity, missing recording an event by mere seconds, has happened too many times to ignore the pattern by now. I cannot help but wonder at the theory that we are not meant to record these paranormal experiences. Does our distraction or vulnerability at rest play a part in its mani-festation somehow? Is it only meant to be experienced viscer-ally in the moment, not a watered-down recording to show others?

Whatever it was, as frustrating as it was, nothing from the specific multi-light event was recorded, though I was pleased to have experienced some unexplained activity. It was also fun to see my husband genuinely confused by what was happen-ing. I opened my phone camera to record a brief video noting the event, my voice gravelly with sleep. We eventually got back to bed, nothing further waking us from slumber.

Upon review of all my abandonment footage, as predicted, I couldn't use any of the audio due to the street noise. There was no movement in the room, and though I was able to capture some random K2 hits while we slept, that alone isn't much to get excited over without a separate corroborating device hit or other experience. I will note that the K2 didn't constantly react all night long, but as always, I take a solo K2 hit with a grain of salt, as both the natural environment and other electronic devices in the room can easily affect it.

The Hotel Bethlehem is absolutely beautiful, with delightful amenities and service. I get the sense that the 3 a.m. light show was significant – a tease. Next time, it's you and me, room 932.

CHAPTER 29

THE SUN INN

BETHLEHEM, PENNSYLVANIA

J ust as I enjoy random macabre trips, sometimes my husband and I will follow a random interest as an excuse for a little daytrip together, to break up the monotony of daily parent life. If our schedule allows, it doesn't take much for us to find an excuse to go on a mini adventure – sometimes we will travel to a destination just to dine at a restaurant of a celebrity chef we like, or to see certain filming locations, like when we trekked up and down Manhattan to visit sites seen in *Ghostbusters*.

On one recent adventure, we were on a quest to acquire the historical spirit (as in alcoholic beverage, in this instance) cherry bounce. Cherry bounce is a type of moonshine we learned about from a reality series we watched obsessively one spring. I don't even remember why we started watching it, but when we heard that this particular liquor was hard to find, we sensed a challenge. We like trying interesting cocktails together, and I became even more interested in trying it after I learned that it had a historical significance, having been George Washington's favorite drink. It's said he wouldn't travel without a flask of his wife Martha's cherry bounce recipe on his person. Oh, George, you big softie.

Current laws in Pennsylvania prohibit moonshine (even legal moonshine) from being shipped directly to our address, so it was up to us to make our way to a distributor. I was thrilled when we found that the closest distillery specializing in cherry bounce was located in Bethlehem, Pennsylvania, one of our favorite haunted towns. It's the same town where we had an interesting overnight experience at the Hotel Bethlehem not long before. Coincidentally, the tavern that sold the liqueur was located inside a historic haunted property. The trip seemed meant to be.

The Sun Inn dates back to 1758 and was a popular accommodation during Revolutionary War times. Its guest list frequently included such notable names as George and Martha Washington, Ben Franklin, John Adams, Samuel Adams, Ethan Allen, and Alexander Hamilton. The claims of hauntings on the property include sightings of a nurse named Elizabeth Moore, who died there in 1897, her spirit appearing in nurse garb with a strained expression. It's said to also be haunted by a more modern entity, one Hughetta Bender, a Sun Inn Preservation Association founder who cared deeply about restoring the historic building.[38] Rarely do I hear ghost stories where the spirit in question is a familiar face to those witnessing the activity. I was very interested to visit.

In the end, my visit was brief but productive; we popped in to sample the sought-after cherry bounce, finding the bar room set just off the stairwell on the second floor. It was delicious, incidentally, a full, deep cherry flavor muddled with intense winter spices. The broad stairwells beckoned me upward as we made our way to the little bar room, and I swiveled my neck in every direction to take in the old-fashioned décor. Large portraits of George Washington and other political figures and war heroes hang along the walls. Over-sized painted wooden doors creak on their hinges while the scuffed floorboards groan in response. The rooms manage to feel creepy despite the sunshine pouring in the many windows onto whitewashed walls. I was able to peek around a bit on our way through the museum, but we didn't have time to stay for the proper tour they offer on-site. As I love Bethlehem so much and have barely begun to graze the surface of all its spooky secrets, I fully intend to stop by again soon and enjoy a meal at the tavern, beyond a mere quick cocktail.

CHAPTER 30

SALEM PIONEER VILLAGE

SALEM, MASSACHUSETTS

I t seems egregious not to mention Salem in my compiled list of macabre destinations, though my trip there was not specifically paranormal in intention despite having traveled with fellow paranormal investigators. The trip was meant to be a girls' weekend full of shopping and dining, and it most definitely was, but of course, we couldn't help but find our way to some spooky stops. This was my second visit to Salem, having visited there while on a work trip to Boston some ten years prior. That visit was only a handful of hours, zipping by myself to the Witch Museum and up and down Essex Street before hastily departing as night fell and the early October crowd started filing in. This recent trip with friends was in the midst of a few beautiful July days – Salem in the fall is gorgeous but crowded, and there's something about Salem in the bright summer sunshine too.

I don't think I need to go too in-depth over the history of Salem and its ties to the Witch Trials of 1692, piracy in Colonial America, or its current magnetic pull for Halloween fanatics. It's a version of Mecca to the spooky community. Salem is undoubtedly a special place. We visited so many wonderful little shops along and near Essex Street, selling all manner of crystals and incense, candles and interesting books. I discovered my new favorite candle store just across from "the Witch House" and the Ropes Mansion. I posed with the famed *Bewitched Samantha* statue. We ordered lobster rolls at recommended restaurants and enjoyed too many dry martinis at a concert in the basement of a gem of a bar we found accidentally.

To my unending delight, I was able to convince my friends to hightail it out to the site of Max and Dani's house on the bay from the movie *Hocus Pocus* and see a nostalgic Halloween home in person. The home used in the film is conveniently located just next to another site they used in the movie, the Salem Pioneer Village.

The Old Salem Pioneer Village was used as the set for the character Thackery Binx's village in *Hocus Pocus*, but was never actually an old historic village, merely a living history museum for visitors to experience early seventeenth-century life. Though we knew it was only a replica, we thought we could use the village as a sort of giant trigger object, together with water energy from its proximity to the bay, to try a makeshift Estes session. The village wasn't yet open to visitors, so we found ourselves alone outside the gates on some wooden benches, caressed by the breeze from the sea. I put the SB-7 headphones in and turned the device on, though I wasn't using proper noise-canceling headphones and could hear my friends' questions. We had been in Salem a full day by that point and hadn't tried to connect with spirit in any way, so we thought it would be worth it, even imperfectly. It is my opinion that we were right.

The session began slowly, obvious voices from nearby radio stations coming through in steady, recognizable intervals. After a few moments, I started to repeatedly hear the voice of what sounded to be a young man. As I could hear my friend's questions, I can't deny any bias heavy with my own apophenia, the tendency to perceive a meaningful connection between random bits of information. However, even in trying to stay the course of saying only what I heard, there did seem to be a halting back-and-forth dialogue coming through. My friend, a psychic, connected with first a young man who worked near or with the ocean and ships, and then a woman who may have lost a child.

Most notably, there was a moment when my friend asked, "Do you have a child with you?"

And I heard the voice say, "Not anymore."

These are indeed wild leaps to connect a few responses to a narrative, but that was the general sense of the session. Eventually other tourists arrived, and we wrapped up our experiment before continuing our weekend's adventures elsewhere in Salem.

CHAPTER 31
EASTERN STATE PENITENTIARY
PHILADELPHIA, PENNSYLVANIA

L iving within an hour's drive from Philadelphia places me delightfully close to some major pieces of American history, many of them supposedly haunted. With my regular schedule of wrangling school drop-offs and pickups, feeding everyone, and getting to bed at a reasonable hour, coupled with my distaste for driving Route 76 (potentially a top ten contender for the worst highway in the country), I have yet to explore all the haunted Philadelphia hotspots on my list. I haven't spent nearly as much time as I'd like in the city's many haunted restaurants, hotels, bars, and historical landmarks, though as my children grow, I'm seeing pockets of time open up little by little. I look forward to future explorations. Fortunately, there is one behemoth I was lucky to have visited years before my schedule was wound up so tightly – Eastern State Penitentiary.

My first trip to Eastern State was years ago, in 2007. I graduated college, and my favorite cousin traveled from Colorado to attend my graduation ceremony and stay with me for a few days. I retroactively and publicly apologize to her here for the blow-up mattress on which she had to sleep in my dilapidated apartment – being newly graduated does not make for the finest of accommodations. She had always been my spooky partner-in-crime, loving paranormal shows and ghost stories as much as me, and we knew we had to tour Eastern State in her time on the East Coast. We arrived at the penitentiary and stared up at the fortress of the outer walls – a veritable medieval castle plunked down in a major city – and we were not disappointed.

Eastern State Penitentiary is one of the most famous historic prisons in the country, known for its then-innovative "wagon wheel" design, in which an octagonal center room was connected by corridors to seven radiating cell blocks, so the warden or guard on duty in the center room could theoretically monitor all the blocks at once. ESP housed such notorious criminals as Al Capone, whose cell was notably and suspiciously more luxurious than any other in the prison, complete with tapestries and the warm light of a lamp gleaming off a burnished wood desk.

Eastern State was one of the first prisons to encourage separate prisoner incarceration, keeping prisoners apart as part of their rehabilitation plan. Each cell was concrete, with only a small door and a single glass skylight, meant to symbolize the "Eye of God," suggesting God was always watching them. The isolation enforcements were intense. Even when an inmate left his cell, a guard would wrap a terrifying-looking white hood over his head to prevent any interaction or recognition between inmates. The worst-behaved prisoners were put into a pit called "the Hole," an underground cellblock where they would have no light and only minor human contact at mealtimes, for as long as two weeks. The extreme measures imposed on inmates was the opposite of helpful, driving many prisoners to their mental limits and inciting hostile behavior between guards and within the prisoner population regardless of isolation efforts.

The prison also employed various types of punishments, including periods of induced starvation; the water bath, when inmates were dunked in a bath of ice-cold water and then hung from a wall for the night; or the "Mad Chair," where inmates were strapped tightly to a chair, restricting any and all movement for days on end. Although executions were not carried out at Eastern State, the prison was home to its fair share of murders. At least two guards were murdered over the years, as were many inmates. Hundreds of others died from disease and old age in the system.[39]

The prison was closed in 1971, after it was designated a National Historic Landmark in 1965. It was abandoned for many years and sat in ruins until 1988, when the Eastern State Penitentiary Task Force began to offer historical tours of the property. Since 1994, historical tours have been offered on a daily basis, attracting close to 220,000 visitors each year. In 1991, the first Halloween fundraiser was held, and has been every year except during the Covid-19 pandemic.[40] The Halloween attraction used to be a standard jump-scare haunted house, but has recently transitioned to a less intense, eerily lit history-based tour and beer garden.

That day all those years ago, my cousin and I began our self-led audio tour of the grounds, marveling at the enormity of the decaying corridors of cell after cell, giggling as we spooked ourselves every few feet. I think we both hoped we'd see something unexplainable. Eastern State has no shortage of paranormal claims, and a popular ghost-hunting show had recently filmed there. As a matter of fact, the gift shop at Eastern State was selling DVD sets of the show in question, and purchasing it probably lit the flame for my paranormal TV obsession over the following few years.

I had heard plenty of ghost stories about the site and could easily envision each of them taking place, surrounded by peeling plaster walls around me, thrown into relief by skylights and wire mesh dividers above. Angry growls in visitors' ears, shoves by phantom hands, choking sensations by unseen attackers: it all seemed possible here. Interestingly, most claims were from visitors on tours like ours, in broad daylight. Sadly, the penitentiary no longer offers private overnight investigations, but even on a sunny day like the day I was there, the energy within the walls is heavy, waiting with intent. Stepping into each cell felt like a previous inmate was sitting right there beside you, judging you for your intrusion, and considering letting you know it.

There's an interesting restaurant literally across the street from the penitentiary – a refurbished fire station, to be exact. When our tour ended, I was grateful to freely leave the prison and head to lunch there, shaking off the phantom touch of angry fingers. The hostess sat us at a table perched right on the street facing the prison, its massive walls shooting straight up in a giant stone curtain beside us. Even then, it felt as though the spirits inside that fortress somehow watched me where I sat, just outside their reach.

CHAPTER 32

PHILADELPHIA ZOO

PHILADELPHIA, PENNSYLVANIA

Historic prisons, grand hotels, former speakeasies... a zoo? Though not exactly one of the first locations that comes to mind when conjuring up the idea of spooky places, the Philadelphia Zoo is, in fact, haunted, according to some of its many employees. I have been intrigued by the paranormal claims centering around the Philadelphia Zoo ever since it was featured on a prominent ghost-hunting show years ago. Until then, I had never conceived of a zoo as being haunted, though I don't see why it couldn't be, especially given its history and location within such a prominently historical city. I'd been for a few visits before I had children, and again when my kids were younger, but at that point I was focused on dispensing snacks and taking memorable photos with gorillas in the background. Once my kids could reapply their own sunblock and last longer between restroom breaks, my attention was slightly freed up so that on my recent trip, I could try to suss out some of the paranormal claims (and *also* take photos of gorillas).

The Philadelphia Zoo, America's first zoo, opened its gates

on July 1, 1874, after the Civil War delayed its original opening plans by fifteen years. It was the first zoo in the world to develop specially formulated foods for zoo animals, and the first children's zoo in the United States. The Philadelphia Zoo was also the first to open an animal care and research laboratory on-site in 1901: the Penrose Research Laboratory, which contributed to a reduced rate of disease and longer lifespans of the animals. This lab was under the leadership of Dr. Charles B. Penrose and Dr. Cortland Y. White, professors at the nearby University of Pennsylvania. Also on the grounds are the administrative buildings, the John Penn House and the Shelly Building.[41]

Unfortunately for paranormally inclined zoo-goers like me, it is not the visitors' sections of the zoo that are said to be the most haunted. While there are scant reports of the Children's Treehouse building having some poltergeist-type activity, the hotspots seem to be in the employee-only offices and administration buildings. Employees at the zoo often report claims of flickering lights and odd sensations all throughout the zoo grounds, but apparition sightings have occurred mostly in the Penn House, the Penrose Building, and the Shelly Building. Specifically, in the Penn House, sightings have occurred of a woman's ghost standing at the top of the stairs, as well as disembodied voices and footsteps. In the Shelly Building, visitors to the zoo report a face peering through the windows in the lobby, and in the Penrose Building library, reports of a female apparition have been seen. I haven't read any reports of ghost animals.

The zoo shields well its administration buildings from the eyes of zoo guests. While it's meant to be aesthetically pleasing and keep the focus on the wonderment of the animals around you, it's comically frustrating for a ghost enthusiast trying to sneak a peek at the haunted buildings on-site. I craned my neck to peer over the tarped fences as best I could, but at five feet three inches and dragged along by two excited kids, I had very little time to gaze and attempt to connect with anything of the spooky variety. So it appears that unless I quickly work toward a degree in veterinary science, I will likely not get my desired one-on-one time with the zoo's spookier attractions.

After our zoo visit, I convinced my family that on the way home, we should stop for refreshments at one of my favorite city restaurants – the refurbished fire station across from Eastern State Penitentiary. I thought my kids would enjoy the décor there, complete with fireman's pole. The fact that I wanted to return there because it is literally across the street from the towering stone walls of the penitentiary only factored in *slightly*. Can I be blamed for wanting to be near two haunted locations in one day? We requested outdoor seating, and I sat in the courtyard, sipping an ice-cold raspberry-rum concoction on that warm day, a breeze ruffling my hair as my kids played in the small patio fountain. As I gazed up at the stone edifice across the road, enjoying both my cheerful family and my proximity to the ghosts I am sure were just beyond those walls, I felt peace.

It's days like these, spent with my family, dabbling in both a bit of wholesome fun balanced with a bit of spooky, that make me feel refreshed. I get so excited when my children are as intrigued as I am about my ghost stories as we go about our activities. It's unusual, yes, but for that reason it makes our outings unique and special. It's like a choose-your-own-adventure each time we go somewhere new as a family. It's a life lesson in embracing being different and seeing the world through a different perspective.

When my children are teenagers – brief pause as I shudder at the thought – I'm sure my interests will be "lame," or whatever derogatory lingo is used at that time, and I'm trying to mentally prepare for that. But maybe, if they come back around after their angsty years, they'll see that I was always trying to add an interesting facet to our days. I am always reaching for more to enrich my own day-to-day. In doing so, I've found I have more resiliency, more reasons to stay positive and open-minded when the tough times inevitably come. If your interests are varied and you throw yourself into them because they matter to you, there will always be more directions to turn to for inspiration, creativity, study, excitement, or even just distraction. So until they put up a cogent argument otherwise, I will continue dragging them to the spooky spots on my ever-growing list. At the least, perhaps their grades in future history classes will benefit.

CHAPTER 33
POTTSGROVE MANOR
POTTSTOWN, PENNSYLVANIA

O ne random drizzly morning in the summer of 2021, my car found its way to the Pottsgrove Manor Historic Site. The humidity gave me an awkward stifling hug as I stepped out of my car, but even still, this building really caught me off guard when I pulled up. It is not well known, even in the area, despite the recent flurry of historical events and social media efforts of its preservation society, and I thought my kids would enjoy the free tour. The manor doesn't have any kind of openly discussed paranormal reputation per se, yet on our walkthrough with a very chipper, knowledgeable (and patient) young guide, I was hit in the chest with a sense of spirit nearby, particularly in the enslaved servants' quarters.

The history of Pottsgrove Manor truly begins long before a home was ever constructed on the land. Archaeological excavations on the Pottsgrove Manor property indicate a native presence reaching back thousands of years, likely the Lenape tribe of Native Americans, who used it as a camping location. In 1735, the tract of land that encompasses Pottsgrove Manor was granted to George McCall by William Penn's son, of which an iron merchant named John Potts purchased 995 acres. The main house was built around 1752. Only four acres currently remain of the original 995, so modern visitors see very little of what was then considered a major plantation. The property once had a blacksmith, various barns, two grist mills, a sawmill, and various other small structures dotted across it.

After John Potts's death in 1768, the manor house was purchased by John's eldest son, Thomas, who then sold it in 1783 to Francis Nichols. Although the house moved out of the hands of the Potts family, they were integral in founding the town of Pottsgrove, which was later renamed Pottstown, one of the major local towns in the area to this day. The house and surrounding property were divided and sold several more times over the ensuing years. The manor house itself functioned as a farmhouse, a hotel, a boardinghouse, and an apartment building before being restored and opened as a museum in 1952.[42] With so many hundreds of years of so many lives lived in so many different ways on the property, it is difficult to imagine the manor without a haunting presence.

I tried to set aside my paranormal focus and enjoy the tour, and I was incredibly impressed by both the kindness and breadth of knowledge of our tour guide and the period actors on-site. As we walked through the rooms, my kids enjoyed seeing the old kitchen, with its wide, open hearth and bundles of herbs suspended to dry. As we moved up a back stairwell and into what was once the sleeping quarters for enslaved labor, that old tingly feeling hit me. Even my son abruptly looked up at me and whispered, "Does it feel spooky in here to you?" I nodded and held his hand. He wasn't afraid, just interested. He's so cool.

There were a few bedframes and some cots made up on the floor to illustrate the sleeping arrangements of the time. A few historic items were encased in displays around the room, and a dim shaft of light shone through the solitary window. As my kids and I listened to our guide explain the various duties of the workers, I felt as though something was hovering to my left side, watching us. I couldn't help but quietly ask her if there were any ghost stories attributed to the property. Her expression told me enough, she said they sometimes heard strange sounds, but it's not an aspect of the property they want to encourage. I pressed a little further, mentioning my visits to another historic property, Selma Mansion, about twenty minutes away. She looked a little uncomfortable and added that they'd had trouble with paranormal groups in the past, so I didn't continue my questioning.

We ended the tour in the gift shop, where I bought my kids wooden toy swords and a vintage 1700s-era cookbook (penance for my nosy questions), and gave her my card with contact information. I followed up a week or so later to ask after paranormal overnight bookings, but never received a reply. I'm retroactively furious with whichever other spurious paranormal team was granted access and subsequently burned the bridge for further research by others. I fully understand the historic society's choice to not focus on the paranormal aspect of the building, though it's a shame. I must remember that historical societies focus on historically accurate education regarding their corresponding locations, and *I* am the odd one out, looking for the paranormal twist.

Another beautiful historical site without much paranormal fanfare, perhaps unfairly so, is not too far from Pottsgrove Manor: Fonthill Castle in Doylestown, Pennsylvania.

CHAPTER 34
FONTHILL CASTLE
DOYLESTOWN, PENNSYLVANIA

I n the enchanting town of Doylestown in Bucks County, Pennsylvania, is a most surprising building that seems to appear out of nowhere – a castle. A bona fide towering castle complete with leaded windows and turrets. This extraordinary building, Fonthill Castle, is the brainchild of Henry Chapman Mercer, an anthropologist and tilemaker who lived in Doylestown in the late 1800s. He attended Harvard and studied law at the University of Pennsylvania, though his true passion was in anthropology and archaeology, particularly in the study of ancient tools. He published a great many books on ancient tool making, paleontology, architecture, and engineering, though arguably, his greatest passion was ceramic tilemaking. He traveled Europe extensively and devoted himself to the study of German pottery, for which he is known all over the world.

I visited the castle grounds at Christmastime with my daughter and mother-in-law, when there were thirteen beautifully dressed Christmas trees on display throughout. It made for a very festive, yet simultaneously eerie visit. The castle is almost immediately overwhelming with detail of design as you enter. Stacks of books, framed art and letters, and Moravian tile covers nearly every surface from floor to ceiling in every room, and no single room fits the traditional expectation of what a room should be. As stated on the site's official website: "[the castle is] a window into Henry Mercer's unique architectural and artistic vision, this poured concrete estate is comprised of 44 rooms, 18 fireplaces and more than 200 windows."[43] He built the castle from the inside out; he envisioned rooms he wanted, then found a way to fit them all together. He literally fashioned out of clay each room he wanted in his home in miniature, then pressed the small clay rooms together to create the model for the home he built. This unusual process led to interesting and unexpected sets of steps, interior windows into other rooms, congested hallways, vaulted ceilings, and more. It also creates the feeling that in the dark of night, a turn around any corner could surprise you with a ghostly visage.

After learning more about the man behind the castle, I was fascinated by his intense interest across so many fields of study. The entire castle feels like a love letter to his studies. His piles of books whispered to me to rifle through them, picking one to bring to a cozy chair near one of the soaring windows, but I managed to keep my hands to myself on the tour through the labyrinthine building. Near the end of his life, Henry Mercer wrote another book that strayed a bit from his usual scholarly pursuits, entitled *November Night Tales*. This book was a volume of six short stories (with another story found among his personal papers, added to the volume posthumously), each with a supernatural or gothic theme, including tales of werewolves and one about a sinister crystal ball.[44] I can almost picture him bent over the pages in a corner of his castle, scribbling away scary tales by candlelight.

My absolute favorite room on the tour is Mercer's study, where he had five worktables near different windows so he could follow the natural light through the day as he worked. That room also happens to have on display a human skull, presumably there for educational purposes.

Mercer passed away on the property in 1930 from Bright's disease and myocarditis in an upstairs bedroom. After walking through the building, it is painstakingly clear that Mercer had deep affection and care for the building and the staff who helped him run it all. Every nook and cranny is an ode to a beloved object, theme, part of the world, or his pet dog, who has his very own staircase labeled in lettered tile. It is difficult to adequately portray the home in words and even photos; it just engulfs you where you stand, your eyes darting from the framed landscape hanging an inch from the crown of the ceiling to the artful tile sunk into the floor just under your boot.

Viewed through a paranormal lens, it is honestly hard to believe Henry Mercer would vacate, even after death, the home he poured so much into. In particular, there is a second-floor landing in which two stairwells and two hallways converge. As our guide spoke, I had the sense of someone standing just behind me, then suddenly moving away down the hallway as I turned to look. In a true investigation, a vague inkling like that wouldn't mean very much, but it was a notably odd moment in an odd building. I suspect the room containing the bed in which Mercer passed away may also hold some lingering energy. I'd be very interested in attending an evening tour, to see the ceramics and multitude of decorations in each room thrown into relief, shadows dancing across their surfaces.

CHAPTER 35
BALDWIN'S BOOK BARN
WEST CHESTER, PENNSYLVANIA

Once I became more open about my spooky interests, I started receiving suggestions for destinations I needed to add to my list; a friend insisted that I visit the supposedly haunted shop Baldwin's Book Barn, in West Chester, Pennsylvania. In 1934, William and Lila Baldwin first established their used book and collectible business in Wilmington, Delaware. Having a great deal of success, they wanted a larger location. After World War II, they purchased a dairy barn that had been built in 1822 in the Brandywine Valley, and opened it as a bookstore in 1946.[45] It is still in operation. As I pulled into the parking lot, I looked up at the old stone barn façade and made a mental note to text my friend a "thank you" as soon as possible. It's quite a sight, and once inside, the building feels like something out of, ironically, a fairy tale.

Inside, the jaw-dropping structure contains five stories of a seemingly never-ending maze of shelves of books (including rare and out-of-print volumes), maps, and prints. Various chairs of all colors and styles are crammed into quaint corners, with books and published works piled and stacked haphazardly on every conceivable surface, including inside and on top of old wooden milk crates. It's so full of floor-to-ceiling bookshelves and unexpected stairwells that there are maps of the building tacked onto the walls of the upper floors – I unsurprisingly needed to make use of them more than once.

The building has the strangest sense of ethereal architecture as you begin to climb the many stairwells. Somehow, the interior seems to be much larger than it appears from the outside, which is both fascinating and disorienting. I do not have the best sense of direction to begin with, and I found it easy to get turned around, especially after my attention kept snagging on various titles as I passed shelf after shelf. When I was researching the building before my visit, I came across a description that said it was as if the building was made of the books themselves – this hits it right on the nose.

What could make a building full of books even better? Ghosts. The creaking floors and thick glass windows instantly had me scanning every corner for a glimpse of one of the three spirits they say haunt the premises. I half-expected to see eyes peering at me through the spaces between the steps of the stairwells as I climbed. The first spirit they claim to see is a man resting in the chairs of the upper floors, reading a newspaper. Customers have commented to the employees how pleasant the man with the newspaper was as they perused the shelves near him, when no older man had entered the shop that day, and the shop doesn't even sell newspapers to begin with.

The other two spirits that are claimed to be seen are a female and another man, who they believe may be that of the original owners, William and Lila Baldwin. I'm always very cautious about attributing a name to an unidentified spirit on a whim; I do not wish to offend a spirit with the wrong identification or make random assumptions. Surely many people passed through this place, many lives were lived, and we shouldn't assume spirits at a location must be ones we know from written historical record. It seems to be human nature that we want to identify and label the unknown as soon as possible; it helps us feel more comfortable, perhaps.

In any case, I tucked myself into a corner at the end of a long hallway and ran a very brief Spirit Box session. My attention was admittedly divided between listening to the frequencies as they sped by and keeping an eye on my three-year-old daughter, who was exploring the shelves nearby with reckless abandon. For that reason or another, I received no notable results or evidence of the hauntings, though I definitely see the potential to get a creepy vibe in those endless bookstacks and recommend a visit to any fellow bookworm in the vicinity. I certainly left with a few new-to-me books in hand.

CHAPTER 36
FRICK'S LOCK
GHOST TOWN
LIMERICK, PENNSYLVANIA

One frigid morning, my quest to visit weird local destinations led me to Frick's Lock Ghost Town, just a few minutes' drive from my home. This small strip of land, once inhabited by the Lenni Lenape Indians of the Delaware tribe, has seen the highs of a busy flourishing village, to the lows of a crumbling abandoned town, nearly forgotten entirely.

This small patch of land along the Schuylkill River was awarded to William Penn by the British in 1682, as part of his great forty-five-thousand-square-mile parcel, which would eventually comprise Pennsylvania and Delaware. It remained mostly farmland until the first known building, a farmhouse, was built there in 1757. Other houses and buildings were added steadily over the next few decades as the small village grew. Eventually, the nearby canal expanded to sixty-three miles, and the section of canal through Frick's Lock contributed to the growth of Frick's Locks Village as a bustling stopover point and trading post. In 1832, the sizes of the canals were increased to accommodate larger boats. The village even built a twenty-four-hour "convenience" store to supply the needs of the many boatmen and passengers who stopped in Frick's Lock for dinner or to stay overnight for a stagecoach connection.

However, as time went on and modern, easier travel options entered the scene in the 1880s, the canal was drained. It eventually closed permanently sometime in the mid-1920s. Without the canal, Frick's Lock business diminished into meager farming activities, and much of the population began to move away. The nail in the proverbial coffin came in the 1970s, when a nuclear power company obtained the land surrounding Frick's Lock. While the construction of the plant created jobs in the general region, federal regulations prohibit residential use of lands within 2,500 feet of a nuclear generating station. This meant any remaining residents were more or less forced to leave, and the town was left behind, a shell of its former thriving village.[46] It was entered into the Register of National Historic Places on November 21, 2003, and guided historical tours are now permitted.[47]

On the morning I decided to visit, I had my daughter in the car with me, tucked into her car seat with a juice box, probably wondering what weird place I was taking her to this time. It was ferociously cold that morning, and we ended up parked between the seemingly-empty trailer offices of the nearby construction company on whose property I had driven, so I was loathe to get out of the car, nor leave her inside on her own. So I sat in the car at the end of the closed-off road and filmed a short clip of video, explaining the history of the town and its downfall. I wasn't expecting anything paranormal; this trip was more historical in nature. However, as I filmed, my camera suddenly glitched, and all my open apps shut down before the phone turned off on its own. The sudden panic of being without my GPS on some semi-deserted small back road overshadowed any paranormal ponderings on my part. I even wondered if the cold weather had messed with it in some way, but I'd been in my heated car for at least thirty minutes prior, so that didn't seem likely. I tried again and again to restart it (my battery had been full minutes before), but it refused to turn back on.

I didn't like having my daughter somewhere isolated with no phone handy, so I decided to just leave and hope I remembered my way out to the highway while still trying to get my beloved GPS working. It wasn't until I left the compound and parked in a neighborhood about a half mile away, out of sight of Frick's Lock, that my phone came back to life. Everything on it worked fine, as though it had never had a malfunction. At that moment, I was reminded of another time my phone behaved unusually – at Devil's Den in Gettysburg immediately after my friend thought she had seen an anomaly crawling across the road in front of us. In Gettysburg, I had tried to snap a picture, and my phone resolutely refused to work until we were driving away from the spot. This time, I sat in my idling car on the side of the road, opened up my camera again, and quickly shot a little more video recounting what had just happened. I mused whether proximity to the nuclear plant causes cell phone malfunctions. Surely employees at the generating station use their mobile phones every day, not to mention the company on whose property I was would have settled a little farther away if that was the case. So I allowed myself to consider spookier explanations. The haunting claims are few and far between for this odd but notable location, and I would never immediately correlate my technical issues to ghostly intervention, but it did make me scratch my head a bit. Perhaps there's more to Frick's Lock than meets the eye.

CHAPTER 37

RHOADS OPERA HOUSE

BOYERTOWN, PENNSYLVANIA

O ne of the local macabre stories that I have researched in detail over the years, and has profoundly captivated me time and again, is the story of the Rhoads Opera House fire tragedy. I stumbled across this bit of local history merely by walking past an old building in a nearby town on my way to the library with my kids. I noticed a memorial plaque affixed to the front of a building that now houses a used bookstore, and I was pulled in by what I read. I paused to read the text, and as I gazed up at the brick building, imagining the events unfolding, something inside me became transfixed. It's a story that consistently rises to the forefront of my mind, and I have written various articles for several outlets about the terrible night depicted on that plaque.

The tragedy of the Rhoads Opera House fire happened on January 13, 1908, in Boyertown, Pennsylvania. On that awful evening, a local church group was performing *The Scottish Reformation* for about four hundred of their loved ones. At the start of the third act, a sharp hissing sound filled the air in the auditorium. An insufficiently trained employee had mishandled the valve on the stereopticon projector he was operating, creating the hissing sound, but it was loud enough to startle the crowd and actors behind the curtain. A few of the child actors peeked out from behind the curtain, searching for the source of the noise, and in doing so, knocked over one of the kerosene lamps lighting the stage. Initially, the small fire onstage caused by the fallen kerosene lamp's spilled contents was nearly extinguished, but when would-be helpful audience members tried to move the kerosene tank away from the flame, an even larger spill crested the tank, and chaos ensued.

In the moments that followed, while many increasingly alarmed audience members waited in their seats for the flames to be put out by employees, they should have been hastening their exit from the doomed building. All too quickly, the building proved its many safety deficiencies for such a catastrophe.[48]

As precious minutes passed and panic rose, the mass of frightened people pressed toward the doors, preventing them from opening inward. Those who did make it down the stairwell found that the walls narrowed at the bottom, and the frenzy of people trying to flee wedged together too tightly to escape. Those who remained trapped upstairs found, to their doubtless horror, after fighting through the chaotic maze left by discarded folding chairs from the fleeing audience, that the windows were too high up from the ground to climb through, as the billowing smoke and flames from the stage raged toward them.

There was little to stop the subsequent engulfment as the chaotic scene of hopeless attempts to flee played out. Local fire companies reached the building quickly, but larger crews did not reach the building until hours later. The roof caved in around midnight. The inferno wasn't quenched until the hours of the early morning, and the first bodies weren't recovered until 9 the following morning. The losses were staggering: 171 people died; 29 had been burned beyond recognition. Ten percent of the town's population perished in one night.[49]

Picturing the circumstances of that evening grieves me dreadfully each time I recount them. The panicked fear of the children onstage, the absolute horror of their mothers and fathers, witnessing every parent's worst fear realized in front of them, and the subsequent acute sorrow of the close-knit small community brings a lump to my throat. As a paranormal investigator, I read and research and explore tragic death as part of my everyday, but somehow this tragedy, probably owing to its proximity to my own home where I live with my children, has gripped me time and again since I first began researching it.

Though the tragedy quickly prompted statewide changes in fire safety laws, which no doubt prevented potential future loss of life across the state, the community mourned for weeks after that night. The January ground was frozen solid, and digging graves was taking longer than was desirable, but crews worked to dig a massive memorial in the frozen ground for the unrecognizable dead. In the interim, however, charred bodies remained in local buildings, including the high school and several local saloons. What were once destinations for laughter and camaraderie now served as makeshift morgues. Claims of hauntings as a result of the fire began circulating mere weeks after the event, when the community was still reeling. Many of these reports continue to this day.

I haven't been able to secure a private investigation evening at one of the involved addresses to investigate for myself, though not for lack of trying; the Opera House building has since been divided into private apartments. The many paranormal claims at the building itself, as well as nearby properties, have me so very intrigued. In a local restaurant I often frequent, there are claims of apparitions seen on the ground floor, barware and purses being flung from their positions, and people feeling physically touched by an unseen hand. A local paranormal group investigated at the behest of the saloon owner in 2013, I was able to contact a member of the team, but the individual confirmed that their team dissolved in 2015 on poor terms, and he no longer had access to their old evidence. This particular restaurant is undergoing renovations at the moment; I have to wonder if this will cause an energy shift and ramp up paranormal activity as the architecture is disturbed. I reached out to several of the businesses on the sites once used as morgues, including the restaurant undergoing renovations, to inquire as to strange experiences, but none responded to the message.

Within the ground floor of the building stands an empty commercial property with a long wall of mirrors facing dust-covered floors. The rumor mill in town suggests that the dance studio once there did not succeed when girls in the children's ballet class were too frightened to attend, having seen ghostly images of children in the studio's large mirrors. A local resident who has lived across the street for many years has said she has often seen a woman in white and heard her declare she is "running late for the show" before dissolving away in the wind. These wild claims are unsubstantiated by me, but fascinating nonetheless. My family rolls their eyes and references it as "Mom's Ghost Building" when we walk by on our way to dinner or to the local coffee shop down the road; my eyes are inevitably glued to its brick façade if I am in the vicinity.

I am pleased to relate that the neighborhood has not

forgotten the memory of those who passed. Each year on the anniversary of the tragedy, a memorial service is held at the cemetery memorial site. I have often made trips to visit the memorial myself to check on its tending; rarely have I found it needing much more than a brief weeding.

Often when we wonder as to the "why" of a haunting, we ponder that perhaps the spirits we are noticing want their stories to be told; they want to be remembered. The town seems to do an impressive job of commemorating and honoring the terrible loss of that evening, but maybe that is not enough. Perhaps it is the individual story of each soul lost that night that needs to be told. Perhaps they do not want to be remembered for their manner of death, but for the life they lived, and in many cases, the potential of what they could have been had they lived the years stolen from them. My heart aches at the thought of so many children lost. Though I've embraced this field and its many tragic stories, I have never been comfortable with stories of child spirits.

I have wondered, on the opposite end of the theory, maybe spirits linger because the event is remembered so vividly that they are not allowed to rest. Do we continuously pull them forward from rest as we recall the tragedy that ended their physical existence? Are we poking around where we oughtn't? I hope not, and in my gut, I don't think we're wrong in our research.

I believe it is right to remember, however painful, events such as the Rhoads Opera House fire tragedy and its victims. My own firsthand paranormal research and experiences have led me to follow the common belief that intensely emotional events project out a permanent impact onto the veil separating our world and that of the Other. As a mother, I hate to ever think a child's spirit is "stuck," so perhaps it is wishful thinking when I theorize that these spirits are just flashes of memory imprinted on the Veil, the often-called residual spirit. I will continue to turn my thoughts to those individuals lost that night and my quest to speak to them through the Veil myself, eventually. Mary Becker, aged ten. Matilda Grabert, aged nine. Wayne Romich, aged eighteen. Ira Shober, aged thirty-four. Edna Moyer, aged fourteen, and many, many more.

CHAPTER 38
VALLEY FORGE NATIONAL PARK
VALLEY FORGE, PENNSYLVANIA

Occasionally, on sunny mornings, I feel the pull to explore Valley Forge National Park. The wide-open fields and expanse of sky above never fail to refresh me. The pathways, busy with runners, bikers, and visitors with dogs on leashes, wind around the area that served as the main encampment grounds of Washington's militia over the winter of 1777, while the British held Philadelphia. Twelve thousand troops and four hundred women and children endured the winter there, and while there was never a battle at Valley Forge, disease killed nearly two thousand of them during the encampment.[50] In the modern day, a walk along the path has views of the remnants of the manmade embankments Washington's troops constructed during their stay. Replicas of military huts are grouped here and there, as well as stone memorials, old schoolhouses, and larger visitor sites such as the Arch and the Memorial Chapel on the far north end of the park.

It took about a year of sporadic leisurely visits, but between drizzly spring mornings, humid summer days, and afternoons when fall was just starting to give color to the tall trees along the path, I have walked every foot of the considerably sized park. On each visit I gave myself a rough area of what ground I needed to cover in that visit, but if my eye caught a different path or I felt compelled to explore elsewhere, I always followed the pull.

In addition to the common ghost stories accompanying historic military sites, including phantom sounds of musket fire and seeing apparitions of soldiers in uniform, there is one very specific and unusual ghost claim associated with Valley Forge. During the Revolutionary War, General "Mad Anthony" Wayne was touted as a brilliant military strategist with a fiery demeanor, hence the nickname. He wintered at Valley Forge with Washington's troops and afterward led many victories in battle. When he died in 1796 at the age of fifty-one, he was buried, per his wishes, in uniform in a simple wooden casket in Erie, Pennsylvania. He remained there undisturbed for twelve years until his family decided his burial was not grand enough to honor such a great war hero. His son, Colonel Isaac, was determined to bring his body home to be buried closer to Valley Forge. However, when they opened his coffin to retrieve his body, they were shocked to see it had not decayed enough for it to be easily transported. Rather horrifyingly, they decided to remove the flesh and clothing from his skeleton to be reburied in Erie, while the colonel brought his father's bones to Valley Forge. As if this weren't already the makings of a ghost origin story if I ever heard one, they lost some of his bones along the four-hundred-mile trek across the state. Ever since this ghastly trail of events, there has been a legend of a uniformed man on horseback traveling along the route, which is now Route 322, seeming to be desperately searching for something.[51] Could it be General Wayne endlessly looking for his lost bones?

I have almost always brought two things with me when I visit Valley Forge: my children and my SB-7. The very first time I listened to the SB-7 on park grounds, I was perched inside one of the replica huts. I heard little, which surprised me; I expected to hear radio snippets at the least. Suddenly, a single word forced its way through: "Father." It is quite a stretch to link a single word and the story of General Wayne's son's life-long regret at moving his father's body, but it gives me a little shiver, nonetheless.

On a later visit, my son accompanied me, and it was the first time I showed him how the Spirit Box worked, as I tried another brief session in a different replica hut. I didn't get much in the way of ghostly response, but what I did get was far more meaningful to me – my son's rapt interest in paranormal equipment – and my delight that it didn't scare him one bit. On the visit after that, he shocked me by asking if he could listen to the SB-7 and ask questions to see if he got any responses. He didn't, for which I'm grateful, to be honest. Another trip had us venturing farther to the southwest of the park and right up the middle into the heart of the encampment site and artillery area, where some lone stone houses still stand, including an old schoolhouse, which served as a hospital at the time of the encampment.

Most recently, we finally made our way to properly visit the Washington Memorial Chapel, an architectural feat of beauty. Those immaculate stone hallways with delicate archways captured my heart, blissfully throwing me into the movie *Ever After*, a film near and dear to my teenage self's heart. The chapel is rumored to be haunted, as well as the nearby Valley Forge cemetery, though on our visit we merely enjoyed the views.

MALLORY CYWINSKI

PAWLING SYCAMORE WITNESS TREE

Another one of the most breathtaking and creepy spots at
Valley Forge feels like a secret. It is a small spot quite a distance
from the center of the park itself, on an offshoot street named
Pawlings Road, behind a few crumbling farmhouses. It is the
Pawling Sycamore, also known as the Witness Tree. A "Witness Tree" generally refers to a tree that is much older than
those around it, its lifetime usually spanning centuries, so that
it is said to have "witnessed" important historical events in its
vicinity. This particular tree is thought by some to be at least
260 years old, in which case it would have been standing at the
time George Washington and his troops wintered at Valley
Forge during the American Revolution.[52]

I dragged my son, on the promise of donuts afterward, to
trek through the woods with me to find the tree I had been told
about by an online acquaintance. One hot summer morning,
he and I bumped this way and that over the gravelly road
before parking outside a gate declaring "emergency vehicles
only past this point." We'd have to go the rest of the way on
foot. I admit I was mildly uncomfortable traipsing through a
solitary wooded area on the edge of civilization, but it wasn't
even 8 in the morning – surely creepy killers slept in, or at least
didn't prowl national parks first thing in the morning, right?
(This was what I told myself as we slipped through the fence,
following the prompts of my phone's GPS.) I'd heard of the tree
and its supernatural claims months prior, and we'd finally
made it here; I was determined to see it for myself before aban-
doning ship and fleeing to the nearest coffee shop.

Vehement witnesses claimed to hear disembodied whispers around the tree or even coming from the tree itself. Many
claimed to feel a strange energy when touching the trunk and
branches. I wanted to see if I felt anything similar.

228

My son and I wandered the path together, the sunlight dappling our shoulders through the leafy canopy above. He was going to be starting school the following week, I tousled his too-long hair, and I felt a moment of gratitude that we could sneak away, just us two. A bunny hopped across the path in front of us; my son mused that he was showing us the way.

Suddenly the crush of trees and bushes opened up, and to our left, a massive, sprawling tree reached toward us across an expanse of lawn. The photos and video I took don't do it justice. The tree measures 174 feet across, and some branches have dropped back down into the earth and taken root for support. And the bunny was indeed scampering into the woods behind the tree as we arrived in the clearing.

My son, a chatterbox by nature, stopped abruptly next to me, and we glanced at each other, exchanging some nervous laughter as we both admitted to feeling a little spooked out by the enormity of the tree. There's just something about it. An old decaying building stands next to the tree, whose branches reach over the roof and beyond. The structure would be obliterated if the tree ever fell, but it feels somehow as if that would never happen. Curls of fallen bark litter the ground around the tree like giant confetti. I made my way to the massive trunk in the center. I laid my hands on its bark and had the oddest sensation to say hello and introduce myself, and so I did. I turned toward my son, and as I did, I began to feel a little dizzy, which by now I usually interpret as one of my body's reactions, its "tells," if you will, to nearby paranormal energy. It didn't feel negative or as though we were in any kind of danger; it was as though the tree recognized a curious being nearby and gave me a little ethereal poke. A quiet hello from one of Tolkien's Ents.

We spent some time exploring; my son and I each climbed one of the sturdy branches splayed across the field, until I looked down and realized we were each about seven feet up in the air, and I wasn't under him in case he fell. Thankfully, we both disembarked safely. We verbally asked the tree if we could take some of the fallen bark with us; the curl now sits on my bookshelf amongst other spooky souvenirs I've obtained through the years. I didn't hear any voices, but the impression the tree made on both me and my son leaves me thinking there might be something to its tales. We said goodbye to the tree, and we set off to find my son his sugar-laden reward, as promised.

Valley Forge and its potential spirits will always be special to me for my visits there with my children. I hope that through the years, if there are spirits there, they recognize me for my dedication and respectful intent.

CHAPTER 39
THE CONGRESS HOTEL
CHICAGO, ILLINOIS

While I've consistently found that repeat visits to the same premises unlock a certain level of exponential paranormal activity, sometimes a new location will waste no time in asserting its creepy authority. Such was the case when I visited the Congress Plaza Hotel.

My husband and I celebrated our ten-year anniversary by booking a whirlwind trip to Chicago. Once plans were finalized, I, of course, turned to my friends in the paranormal community and said, "Ok, tell me the spooky spots." Even if the getaway is meant for romance and relaxation, you can bet I am sneaking in a brief spooky side stop in a new place. I can't pass up the chance to see things for myself; it invigorates me. Sometimes a recommended or anticipated spooky spot will inspire that curl of delicious dread in your belly, and sometimes it falls flat. In either case, you've seen it for yourself – you are now a primary source on how it feels to be there. To those of us who cannot easily travel as much as we prefer, we savor these trips and little moments, soaking up the details of the visceral experience.

On our second day in town, after grabbing a delicious apple pie latte, my patient husband escorted me on a long walk to the notorious Congress Hotel. So many of my spooky friends insisted I stop by the historic building, which was already on my radar for a multitude of reasons. Friends shared frightening stories of investigations at the hotel, seeing black masses disappear through walls and even physical assaults by unseen forces to the point of blacking out. The building is absolutely teeming with ghost stories, and I wanted a peek, even if we didn't book rooms there. I've said it before, but I'll reiterate – I've learned to trust my gut. Whether it's motherhood instincts or a habit ingrained from paranormal investigations, when I feel something is "off," I pay attention, even if there's nothing tangible to prove it. Yet.

Stepping through the sliding doors of this building, I was (figuratively) hit in the chest with a feeling of negativity. I am not the kind of paranormal enthusiast who claims demonic activity at every other location, nor am I classifying the Congress Hotel in this category. But there is a thickness to the air in this hotel that I now know would never allow me to actually book a room and stay here on a trip meant for pleasure and romance.

The hotel was originally constructed in 1893 and called the Auditorium Annex, to house visitors flocking to Chicago's famed World's Fair. Additions were added in 1902 and 1907, and by 1911, it boasted over one thousand guest rooms and was renamed the Congress Plaza Hotel. Gilded accents and sparkling chandeliers absolutely dominated the interior décor, drawing in the likes of high Chicago society. After its brief use during World War II as a training school for the army, it returned to its identity as a swanky hotel. It has been popular quarters for presidents through the years and served as an arena for many political conventions.[53] However, the glitz and glam of affluence haven't concealed the many dark tales of this elegant building.

This building has so much dark history, it feels as though the air inside is barely containing it, pushing outward toward the walls. A brief recap doesn't do each ghastly story justice. There are at least three documented suicides in the building, and probably more, each of whose spirits have been claimed to be sighted. Ghosts of brides and grooms are seen in the Gold Room ballroom, sobbing or wandering aimlessly.

There is the well-documented tragic tale of a Jewish refugee mother throwing her sons and then herself out a twelfth-story room window after having to flee Nazi Czechoslovakia. Not only is the door to that particular room now permanently sealed, but it's said her older son's spirit is now seen roaming the hallway on the twelfth floor.[54,55]

Another common tale, though undocumented, is that of " Peg Leg Johnny," a homeless man who was supposedly brutally murdered after being lured to a room on the seventh floor. His spirit is often seen in the lobby and in guests' rooms. Another undocumented legend is that of a woman who plummeted to her doom when the elevator free fell six stories down to the basement. Her ghost is said to haunt the same elevator in which she died. It's said she was on a romantic vacation with her husband, just as I was.

It is even rumored that H. H. Holmes, the country's first serial killer and mastermind of the now-demolished "Murder Castle," just miles away, used to stalk new victims in the lobby of the Congress Hotel. Some claim to have seen his apparition throughout the hotel, wearing a cloak held up to his face.

Most notably, the Chicago Mob boss Al Capone was rumored to have made his headquarters in the building. His spirit is often seen confidently strutting down the corridors on the eighth floor of the North Tower, wearing his finest suit.

Employees of the hotel say that room 441 is the culprit of most guest complaints of unexplainable events, such as objects moving and doors slamming. Paranormal investigators interested in staying in room 441 must book their stay months in advance due to its popularity for consistent activity.

All in all, even one or two of these gruesome stories might constitute enough of a ghost story to act as a magnet for the paranormal community, while simultaneously deterring the average vacationer. With such an incredibly long list of varied claims, however, I am forced to consider whether they are all feeding off each other. Is an individual, upon hearing so many spooky tales, primed in advance to experience something creepy? Or in another light, does the amalgamation of so many dark tales and subsequent hauntings originate from collective thought? Thinking back to the concept of thoughtform hauntings, is the Congress Hotel another potential spot where an egregore may be in play? With so many curious minds turning their thoughts toward this one location, it is a definite possibility, if you subscribe to the idea of an egregore. Or maybe it just really is that haunted. This location is one that draws me in the further I research it. Chicago is already calling me back for another visit.

CHAPTER 40

FORT WILLIAM HENRY (AND A HAUNTED VACATION HOME?)

LAKE GEORGE, NEW YORK

I am forever a lake and mountain girl at heart, having grown up spending summers on the south shore of my beloved Lake Tahoe in California. Living on the East Coast as an adult, however, if I want a lakeside vacation with my family within driving distance, we are heading north to the Adirondacks. One summer in June, we found ourselves vacationing on the shores of beautiful Lake George in upstate New York. Apart from the glittering water, delicious food, and fresh mountain air, I loved the idea of visiting Fort William Henry. Though, before I even reached the haunted fort, I was surprised by an additional spooky space – our rented home for the week.

My family and I had rented an historic home for the week, and I knew almost within minutes of arriving that we had accidentally rented a haunted house for our family vacation. I will keep its location private out of respect for the homeowner, though I dare say she knows full well how spooky the house is. Creaking floors, polished dark wood banisters, framed vintage photos, and an old record player in the living room lent a certain old-fashioned feel to the place. The kitchen, with its butler's pantry and servants' stairwell tucked at the back, seemed to have a sentient watchfulness, somehow. The old, undersized doorknobs rattled at the slightest nearby step, and one windy night made for slamming windows in every far corner of the house. This is all to say nothing of the dusty attic looming above, nor the congested basement below.

Ever on the lookout for spooky intrigue, I had brought a few pieces of paranormal equipment along, just in case. On our penultimate night in the house, after days of feeling eerie vibes, I decided to set up a video camera and cat ball overnight in one of the "creepy bedrooms" at the end of the servants' hallway we had all studiously avoided all week. Even my big, burly, skeptical husband refused to sleep down there one restless night when he sought a different room so as not to disturb me. Sure enough, around three o'clock in the morning, the cat balls lying on the bed began going wild, on and off, for a period of about fifteen minutes. I had hoped for an EVP accompaniment, but upon evidence review, all was disappointingly quiet. Little did I know the truly creepy moment regarding the house wouldn't come until I'd been back home for a few weeks.

Just outside the bedroom in which I had set up this little abandonment session hung one of the creepiest paintings I'd ever seen, which I had attributed to most of the creep factor for that part of the house. It depicted a sullen-faced girl with unusually sloping shoulders, in a pink dress, clutching a blue doll and pointing downwards at a cat with the same grim expression. I couldn't look at it longer than a second or two; why the owner had chosen this artwork for a vacation home escaped my logic.

Weeks after returning home, I was reading up on Greg and Dana Newkirk's Traveling Museum of the Paranormal and Occult, when to my utter shock, this exact painting from the home suddenly stared back at me from my screen. I was gobsmacked. Fate saw fit to show me that the original of this painting, known as *The Restless Painting*, is included in the spooky museum, apparently for good reason. The painting reportedly throws itself, and nearby hanging artwork, off the wall at regular intervals. The Newkirks claim the painting is continually a source for measurable paranormal activity.[56] I have not seen the original with my own eyes, but the coincidence of my having negative feelings toward the copy of the painting and the rooms in its vicinity to the point where I photographed it and discussed it with paranormal friends, then seeing it online a few weeks later was enough to ring alarm bells for me. I hear you, Universe. Was it a coincidence, or something more?

COINCIDENCES, SYNCHRONICITIES, AND THE BAADER-MEINHOF PHENOMENON

I'm probably aging myself in referencing *Seinfeld*, but there's a funny exchange in an early episode in which Elaine is arguing with a writer friend about coincidences. Elaine insists there are *big* coincidences and *small* coincidences, while her friend argues that there aren't variations, just coincidences in general. It makes me laugh every time I see it, and invariably, I then wonder at the distinction myself.

Coincidences seem to take on a life of their own in the paranormal community. It's possible that we are all looking for anything unusual or strange to add to our compilation of "Other." I occasionally get the sense, however, from some investigators' phrasing, that they believe coincidences to be some kind of proof that they have uniquely reached some new plane of understanding, some video game-esque "leveling up" above their peers in this spooky pool. It never fails to tempt me to use the eye-roll emoji, even though admittedly, I myself have noticed in my own life the same theme or instance popping up repeatedly in a short amount of time and wondered if it the coincidence was meaningful, as in my situation with *The Restless Painting*. I think it's possible that these moments really are taps on the shoulder from "Other," like a "Hey, pay attention to this," or "You're on the right track here." However, it seems sensible to pull back on the "synchronicities" train, as a whole, before its temptation carries us too far away from common sense.

"Synchronicity" is a term first introduced at large by analytical psychologist Carl G. Jung "to describe circumstances that appear meaningfully related yet lack a causal connection." As we cannot determine a definite cause-and-effect relationship between random variables, as much as we might *think* they are connected, we cannot declare that noticing something more than once is definitively meaningful. Synchronicities are completely subjective, given all the nuances of a person's consciousness at any given time. Before we call synchronicity publicly, or even privately, really, we must all take our medicine and acknowledge the Baader-Meinhof phenomenon.

The Baader-Meinhof phenomenon, or frequency illusion, is a cognitive bias in which, after noticing something for the first time, there is a tendency to notice it more often. We tend to interpret these multiple occurrences by assuming it is suddenly happening or appearing more often, when in reality, it might just be that we are more conscious of it and noticing it more, when it has been there all along.[57] (The unusual name is derived from a West German far-left militant group from the 1970s; the name of the theory itself came about when in 1994, a man named Terry Mullen wrote to a newspaper column saying that he had first heard of the Baader–Meinhof Group and shortly thereafter came across the term from another source and thought it strange.)

238

In the end, it's just a matter of being aware of selective attention bias (noticing things that are important to us and disregarding the rest) and confirmation bias (looking for things that support our hypotheses while disregarding other potential explanations), two scourges of the paranormal world. Following Occam's razor, in that the simplest explanation is probably the correct one, is a good rule of thumb. When the rabbit hole pulls you down so far that you're deciphering things through a lens fogged with "the Chosen One" trope, you probably need some fresh air.

In studying the paranormal, we are forever straddling the lines between empirically tested psychological study, common sense, and following our gut feelings. How can we simultaneously believe in all three? Yet we do. It's that gray area of trusting *some* subjective interpretations and not others that is forever frustrating, yet fascinating. It's that sliver of "what if?" that keeps us in thrall.

FORT WILLIAM HENRY

One sunny morning on our trip to Lake George, we left our spooky rental house and its weird paintings to head to our tour of Fort William Henry, a meticulously recreated fort built from the exact building plans on the site where the true fort existed before it burned down. A huge fan of the film *The Last of the Mohicans*, based on the novel by James Fenimore Cooper, I was ecstatic to visit the fort where the film is set, though was not filmed there. The fort was also recently featured on a paranormal reality show I enjoy, so seeing it in person was a delight for a multitude of reasons. The fort is most famous for its siege by the French and their Native American allies in the French and Indian War in 1757.

The fort held off the attackers for six days, but eventually the fort was overcome on August 9, 1757.[58] After the surrender, some of the 1,600 Native American allies of the French swarmed the fort in search of the booty they had been promised for their assistance. They scalped many of the people they found, and even more gruesome, they proceeded to dig up some of the bodies in the British military cemetery to scalp the corpses, many of whom had died from smallpox. In doing so, they thus brought smallpox back to their home villages. On August 10, the Native American allies of the French, feeling disappointed with the few scalps they had collected, attacked the retreating British not far from the fort, killing and scalping men, women, and children while the French stood by, complacent.[59]

While some say the hauntings at the fort are a result of the incredible terror and trauma of the siege, many deaths also occurred at the fort in the eighteen months it stood before the attack. Harsh military life in close quarters in the 1700s allowed diseases like smallpox to spread like wildfire, to say nothing of injuries from musket backfire and malfunctions of powerful cannons.

As a wild juxtaposition to its vicious history, the day we visited the fort had beautifully clear sunny weather, and I couldn't take enough photos of the sights around me. My family and I enjoyed the guided tour; my son especially liked the musket demonstration. My four-year-old daughter was not so much a fan of the cannon blast or darkness of the casemates, lit only by a red lightbulb. I thought the ambience was just right.

All in all, it was a delight to explore the expanse of the fort, under the blue sky and adjacent to sparkling Lake George, despite knowing what had occurred here 265 years prior. I snapped a photo of a location just outside the gift shop, where black masses are sometimes seen. We trekked down into the powder magazine, where the path contains original stone from the fort during the siege. The stones on which we walked were there when the original walls around the pathway collapsed from French cannon blasts. The soldiers, women, and children who were fleeing that way were trapped while the impacts and chaos of the siege stormed around them. Those stones witnessed it all.

It is not difficult by any stretch of imagination to consider that the fort may very well be haunted. The staff holds regular ghost tours on-site, and I have come to love when an historic site fully embraces their paranormal potential. It gives credence not only to staff members who have had experiences, but honors those spirits who may still linger. I think it would be difficult to seriously investigate the fort in the summer, due to its proximity to the boisterous downtown area, but in the quiet of winter, if you could make it there safely through upstate New York weather, what potential there must be. With its violent history, thousands of previous inhabitants, and close proximity to a large body of water, I'll bet there is something fascinatingly spooky to find.

CHAPTER 41

EAST MARTELLO MUSEUM, HOME TO ROBERT THE DOLL

KEY WEST, FLORIDA

My husband and I have occasionally snuck down to Key West, a gorgeous town on the tip of the Keys brimming with beautiful sights and steeped in ghost stories. Its paranormal claims to fame are what made me want to visit in the first place. We came for the ghosts; we stayed for the cocktails. On our most recent trip, we went to visit our little friend, Robert the Doll.

Robert the Doll currently resides in Key West's East Martello Museum and Sculpture Garden, but he wasn't always there. The possible inspiration behind the *Chucky* movie franchise and other scary doll films, the little sailor doll was once owned by Robert Eugene Otto, an eccentric artist based in Key West. His grandfather gave him the doll upon his return from a trip to Germany when Eugene was a child. The legends around Robert's supernatural abilities began when his owner Eugene was young, often blaming his bad behavior on Robert, coining the oft-quoted phrase, "Robert did it." It is said that Robert absorbed emotional energy around him and his expression sometimes shifted, as well as his position in the room.

Passersby on the street occasionally claimed to see him moving in the windows in his home above, and staff in the home heard giggling or footsteps from the room in which he was kept.[60]

Anyone interested in haunted or creepy dolls has likely heard of Robert and the unusual demand surrounding him: you must not take a photo with Robert unless you ask him first. Those who have had the audacity to snap a photo without permission have found themselves suffering mishap after mishap afterward, including broken camera equipment, troubled air travel, and more. His exhibit at the museum is surrounded by letters mailed to him asking for his forgiveness and retroactively asking permission for the photo they snapped without consent.

While I do not instantly believe any supernatural claims told to me, I am not one to tempt fate when it comes to curses and bad luck, not with my children around. So I have always asked for Robert's permission for a photo. I even greet him as I approach. The exhibit they have set up is distinctly creepy, with hauntingly quiet instrumental music playing in the darkened passage. He sits in the middle of a long hallway, so you have a few minutes walking toward him to contemplate him as you get closer and closer. It really does feel as though he watches you approach, and judges your worthiness as you step closer. He sits innocently enough on a chair inside an enclosed glass case, though staff members are quick to relay stories of him changing positions overnight on his own. I approached the glass and greeted Robert, as I did the first time I saw him years before. My husband and I both asked permission for a photo, took a few, and that was that. I read some of the newer apology letters sent to him. I wrote a thank-you note on the exhibit chalkboard and continued down the hallway through the rest of the museum.

However, this time, as I turned my back on Robert, I really

did feel as though I was being watched, more so than before. It's easy to feel creeped out by the music and mental image of a haunted doll, but despite knowing the fear cues were there, I admit I genuinely felt a little off-balance this time. I'm on the fence about what followed: a few minutes later, as we moved on to the next exhibit, I felt as though a single fingertip rubbed down the back of my left arm, bare in my tank top. I spun around, expecting a heavy cobweb or perhaps a flag or other artifact from a display hanging over me, but there was nothing. My skeptic husband insisted I simply felt a bead of sweat rolling down my arm – Key West is the epitome of humid, especially adjacent to the beach, but I don't think this was the case. I looked back down the hallway, eyeing Robert in his enclosure, and wondered if he was teasing me. I'm not committed to declaring it a paranormal moment, but it was definitely notable and unexpected. And creepy.

Key West in general is a font of paranormal claims. In addition to Robert the Doll in residence, the East Martello Museum also has relics from the grisly tale of Dr. Carl Tanzler, aka "Count" Von Cosel, a doctor who became obsessed with one of his tuberculosis patients, Elena Milagro. When she passed away, he even paid for her elaborate mausoleum plaque, though they were not actually romantically involved in life except in his mind.

The wildest twist to the story is that two months after she died, he stole her body from its resting place, hiding it alternately in his wingless airplane and then his house. He slept next to her corpse every night for seven years, replacing bits of her with various materials, including plaster, silk, and wax, as the body deteriorated. To say this man was unhinged is an understatement. His deeds were finally discovered, and authorities found Elena's decayed body nestled in his bed, dressed in an elaborate wedding gown. Unbelievably, though

Tanzler was initially charged with grave robbing, charges were eventually dropped on the grounds that the statute of limitations had passed, presumably due to Key West wanting to be rid of the media circus that erupted at the discovery of his crimes. He fled the city for another Florida town, where he lived the rest of his years in quiet notoriety, forever unrepentant for what he had done.[61]

Interestingly, on the day he left Key West, Elena's tomb mysteriously exploded. The pieces of her shattered mausoleum plaque are currently on display at the East Martello Museum. Seeing the plaque, and having read so much about this wild macabre tale, I felt pulled to visit the cemetery in which Elena Milagro was originally laid to rest. The tomb had once been in a place with paranormal tales of its own, the Key West Cemetery. This meant, of course, it was time to face my fear of visiting a cemetery.

CHAPTER 42

DEATH, GRIEF, AND CEMETERY EXPLORATION

Before I started investigating the paranormal, I thought people who explore cemeteries in their leisure time were strange, disturbed, or disrespectful. I have learned, however, that these judgmental feelings probably stemmed, as they usually do, from a place of fear. The fear wasn't of the cemeteries themselves; I've been a fan of zombie films for as long as I can remember, and I don't think every cemetery is automatically haunted. It was more a conditioned reaction from younger years of always "looking the other way" when it came to grieving or acknowledging the fact that, eventually, we all must die. It felt wildly uncomfortable to consider meandering a cemetery or graveyard as part of a hobby, even if I regularly speak to the dead.

Death and I did not have a proper introduction, so to speak, though few people do, I suppose. In my mind, Death storms in and takes what it wants, a fearsome beast bent on coming for us all, sooner or later. In my experience, when it left, there was only silence in its wake. But there shouldn't be.

Growing up, while I think my parents were trying their

best, there were a lot of taboo subjects in my family, including the discussion of death. Granted, discussing death and dying is not a fun or easy topic appropriate for everyday discussion, but to ignore it completely and even get angry when it comes up is to deny any comfort with the topic at all. I guess it just boils down to the fact that the paramount emotional "safe space" in my family dynamic was elusive. It wasn't always missing, but I couldn't count on it. I never went hungry, and I never endured physical abuse, but the level of emotional stability in my home was a wild card. Some days I felt like I could talk more freely, that my parents were tuned in and I was comfortable in my home. On many other days, I felt like if I said one errant word alluding to one of our unspoken taboo subjects, I would be in for tears and slammed doors.

Each morning, I awoke and stared up at the glow-in-the-dark stickers on my ceiling as anxiety coiled in my stomach. I never knew if the day ahead would be calm, with family members getting along and the day moving forward normally, or if the hours ahead held uncomfortable resentment bursting into volatile arguments by dinnertime. It was truly a toss-up, and it was my "normal." Living on the edge of my seat day in and day out was turmoil for my already-chaotic teenage emotional threshold. It affected my friendships, confidence, and physical health. When big stressful life events, like a death in the family, occurred and I should have felt and worked through my feelings like a normal grieving person, I instead swallowed them and pushed them down. Adding an actual important event like a death into the mix was adding burning kindling to a constantly smoldering fire.

Ironically, while I wasn't allowed to discuss the deaths of loved ones through the years, my mother frequently and openly discussed her suicidal thoughts with me. She once read me a list she made of "things she could do instead of committing suicide," as though I were her therapist, not her daughter. I can't even comprehend the compartmentalization of the separation of thinking that talking about suicide, but not grief, was acceptable. She would share her thought process on why she considered suicide on a particular day as casually as what her current favorite movie was, but would never discuss losing a grandparent. I just don't understand, even now, why a calm discussion on grief was a hard no in our house. It baffles me, though again, at the time, I thought that was normal.

As parents, we must have the hard conversations with our children, in age-appropriate language. It is our job to be a trusted source of facts and an emotional model, to help our children talk through complicated feelings, and be the stalwart ear for their thoughts and questions as they sort through how they feel. This does not mean we share every thought we have on the topic of death, and certainly not any suicidal ideation we have. There are other far more appropriate resources or audiences for those discussions, like doctors or other adult friends. While addressing the tough topics with our kids is not fun and not easy, it's necessary. Looking back, now raising my own family, I shake my head at how many topics made my parents uncomfortable to the point of ignoring them completely. I missed out on so much dialogue and meaningful conversations with my parents in what should have been a safe setting for me to ask questions and digest my naturally curious thoughts. Setting aside their discomfort then could have made the difference for an honest and healthy relationship now. Instead, I felt I wasn't allowed to freely and comfortably discuss such normal, important topics as religion, puberty, sexuality, and death. Death is scary and uncomfortable, and even as a paranormal researcher often studying tragic death as part of a chosen hobby, too much contemplation of the topic leaves me drained and morose. Yet death is inevitable, and though it is difficult, it is imperative that we discuss it more openly.

My mother lost her brother when I was about eleven or twelve, and that was the first time death touched my life in a real way. I remember feeling like I wasn't allowed to have a reaction to it. My uncle had always been a distantly loving but mysterious member of the family. He lived on the other side of the country and sent cards for my birthday, but that was the extent of our relationship, so I wasn't devastated when he died, but it was still sad and shocking, and I worried for my mother. I was young, and it was the first death that felt real to me. My mother had been close to him, and his death obviously shattered her. I can only imagine how deeply it hurt her, but it was apparent that it was part of the catalyst for her many turbulent years following. Other family members told me to never talk to her about it, and she herself said the same. Even a decade later, as a young adult, I was never allowed to discuss it without her breaking down completely and changing the subject to other, more trivial things. I never had a conversation with her about grief apart from seeing countless tears and her increasingly erratic behavior. I was never asked how I felt when he died, and we certainly didn't broach real discussions about the afterlife, as that looped in a potential mention of religion, another taboo topic in our family. Oddly, we'd watch old ghost movies sometimes or talk about haunted houses, but it always felt detached from real death. The afterlife was entertainment: a distant, imaginary, almost funny topic then; we never discussed our actual beliefs on the matter in honest conversation. In recent years, when she'd heard I'd started paranormal investigating, she would randomly text me, "Say hello to Grandma," sometimes. It was too little, too late, too casual; it always made me uncomfortable. I blankly stared at those messages. I didn't know what to do with them.

Through the years, as aunts and uncles and my grandparents passed away, I was told to "not talk about it... it hurts too much." So I never did. If someone passed away, we seemed to have an unspoken understanding of who was deemed "the most affected person," and we left that person alone and acted like the death never happened. We didn't attend funerals, never mentioned the deceased person, never asked how anyone was feeling, even weeks and months later. I can understand not launching into conversations about death while newly mourning and the pain was raw, but surely years later it can and should be discussed. I understand it wasn't always my place as a daughter to demand immediate openness from my parents, nor to constantly badger them in their grief. I didn't wish to obsess over wretched details, but surely families must come together in grief to tackle it in a healthy way and move forward. If nothing else, we disrespect the memory of the dead by ignoring the fact that we lost them.

Maybe I'm being selfish, expecting too much, pouting that I didn't get what *I* wanted during life-altering moments of loss for those around me. Maybe I'm just jaded regarding my family dynamic in general, and I can't help but see my memories through that tarnished lens. I acknowledge that possibility. However, the way death and grief were managed when I was young left me feeling unequipped to handle it for years to come.

Surely as a mother now myself, I should be able to better understand how difficult it is to be a parent, especially in hard times. And I do. There are other patterns and decisions in my upbringing that I see more clearly now and have forgiven, though I admit I bristled at the moment of comprehension, often finding it easier to lump it all together and lay blame en masse, as immature as that sounds. The fact is when it comes to how conversations about death, grief, and suicidal ideation were managed in my childhood family, I cannot wrap my mind around the choices that were made. I am sure to overcompensate and make plenty of my own errors in parenting, but not when it comes to this.

When two of my classmates died in a tragic car wreck in high school, it was the first time I felt allowed to openly mourn a death. They weren't relatives, so per our unspoken familial pattern, that meant I was "the most affected one," and I was allowed to feel the pain and the loss of their lives, though they weren't close friends of mine. I requested to attend their funerals, and my mother agreed to accompany me to their church services, though we didn't join the crowd at the gravesite afterward. Theirs were the first funerals I ever attended, and I was rocked to my core. They were terrible days, but I don't regret attending and paying my respects, however painful. The depth of devastation coursing through the hallways of my school forever stays with me. I still note them on the date of their deaths, twenty plus years later. Some years, I have woken on that January date feeling resolutely melancholy, and it only occurred to me hours later why I felt such unease; it was as though my body remembered first, and my mind caught up later.

Until a few years ago, I had avoided cemeteries for the most part. They were forbidden and frightening – gravestones were props from horror movies. My feelings were a relic of my childhood, growing up with that strict avoidance pattern. To visit a cemetery was off-limits, unheard of. As an adult, I started to attempt the dismantling of this mindset. When I visited Savannah with my favorite cousin a few years back, we did a quick tour around the famed Bonaventure Cemetery, but somehow the visit felt more like a museum than a burial place that triggered my anxiety. I didn't have the same fear reaction to Bonaventure as I did to cemeteries I passed on daily errands in my hometown. It didn't feel like I'd overcome anything in Savannah, it just felt like a tourist stop of a beautiful sculpture garden. Maybe I'd unconsciously compelled myself to think of it as such.

The first time I actually visited an active cemetery was on the awful day we buried my husband's grandfather. It was after a full day of his wake plus another morning in the funeral home among desperately sad extended family, and I was exhausted from grief, both my own and absorbing that of others. I had no previous experience with the extensive service situation, and it wore me down. I really had no choice but to visit as the ceremony's events proceeded, and I was so lost in the grief of the day and concern for my husband, who was a pallbearer, that I literally barely remember stepping foot in the cemetery itself. Years later, on that trip with my husband to Key West, after reading the story of Elena Milagro and Carl Tanzler, I knew it was time to face my fears and visit Key West Cemetery.

CHAPTER 43

KEY WEST CEMETERY

KEY WEST, FLORIDA

We rented a little golf cart and made our way through the small quiet side streets of the city to the Key West Cemetery. The cemetery, where Elena Milagro's mausoleum had originally stood, has its own paranormal claims, which bolstered my motivation to go. The cemetery holds the remains of one hundred thousand people, more than the number of people living in Key West. One of its claims to fame is its many humorous headstones, including the notorious stone of B. P. "Pearl" Roberts, which says: "I told you I was sick." More soberly, though, it is said to be haunted by a little girl who tries to get you to play hide-and-seek. The far more intimidating ghost story is that of the "Bahamian Woman," who is extremely protective of the burial ground and will become viciously angry and scream in your face if you are disrespectful of the dead. I was determined not to offend her.

We arrived, and I cautiously stepped onto the little stone pathway, trying to be as quiet as I could, out of both respect and nervousness, not for the ghosts, but the location itself. My heartbeat pounded in my ears – I remember not knowing if it was in fact OK that I was there, meandering my way through salt-weathered gravestones in broad daylight. What was the etiquette? My anxiety threatened to take over and steer me back to my little cart in search of a restaurant with loud, happy music and mojitos. That had been what I was used to – an abrupt change of topic when death-related discomfort kicked in. "No," I told myself. I was going to face this.

It was, in fact, an oddly beautiful space, but I couldn't shake my internal awkwardness. I stood at a crossroads of little paths between the headstones, sweating from the sun overhead, mild panic flooding my veins, urging me to flee. At that moment, however, my attention snagged on a jogger casually making his way through the cemetery a few rows over, who gave me a friendly wave as he passed. I lifted my hand in return, and it clicked that my discomfort was merely a lack of experience and the rebellious bucking off of the restrictions I'd felt since I was a child. After that moment of revelation, I was shocked by how peaceful I found the cemetery to be. I found, to my surprise, that I actually felt *more* respectful visiting and reading some of the many headstones than studiously avoiding them and ignoring their existence. I didn't see the little girl or the Bahamian Woman, but the visit was a success on a personal level. I was grateful for it.

Since then, back home in Pennsylvania, I may not have become an avid cemetery explorer, but I have made it a point to visit other resting spots. I even have a favorite cemetery now – yes, I've at least come that far – the cemetery wherein lie some of the unidentified victims from the Rhoads Opera House fire tragedy. I have even taken my daughter on a sunny day or two to visit the memorial marker there, to bring flowers or upright some fallen vases. I've sought out untended burial plots tucked into the edges of abandoned fields and paused at the side of a road to read an interesting headstone in a graveyard. I've read the names on headstones in Salem and taken a moment to reflect. I made a trip out to Lancaster, Pennsylvania, specifically to see the country's first crematorium, which pulled me down a rabbit hole of research on that morbidly fascinating process. Sometimes I look over at my bookshelf and marvel at some of the titles I see there. My younger self wouldn't believe I'd be so openly interested in it all.

On one random sunny day last year, I decided to push the envelope even further and drive to a local cemetery with my SB-7 in hand. An SB-7 scans radio frequencies at a rapid rate, and some investigators believe spirits can manipulate the frequencies to "speak." By that time, I'd had uncanny experiences with it before and honestly, I thought a video of my little experiment would make for interesting content on social media. I think I was right.

When I arrived, there were gardeners at work, and I still wasn't fully at ease with visit etiquette, so I decided to stay in my parked car and run my session. I set my phone into a traveling tripod and hit record. I asked some questions but did not hear much projected back to me. It was about ten minutes into my little experiment that I started to feel strange – I had just asked "Can I bring you anything?" when a gut feeling of discomfort coupled with a wave of dizziness overtook me. I vaguely recognized the feeling as the same physical sensations (though without nausea), I had felt on the battlefield at Gettysburg, when I had the overwhelming urge to escape back to the safety of the hotel.

I decided to wrap up my activity, and I proceeded to drive to a café and purchase a sugary coffee drink to combat my dizziness, thinking I'd just had a minor dip in my blood sugar between meals. I sipped my icy brew as I sat in my car, reviewing the minutes of footage I'd just recorded. Strangely, in my video, at the very moment I started to feel dizzy, a dark shadow appeared to fill my car for a split second. I paused, putting my drink into the cupholder without taking my eyes from the screen, and opened the clip in my video editor. I slowed it down to half-speed, then even slower, certain that I'd see the shadow pass from one side of the car to the other – a sure sign a bird had simply flown over my vehicle and momentarily blocked the sun. What I saw was simply the interior of my car evenly darkened for less than a second. The darkness immediately dissipated. It was a cloudless sunny day, and I didn't remember this occuring, nor do I acknowledge it in the video.

Ordinarily, I would chalk up the visual anomaly to a glitch, but while I'd had malfunctions before, I'd never seen a visual glitch like that, nor did it happen again in the stretch of video. My phone has, on other occasions where I felt something was "off" in a paranormal way, abruptly turned off or had the camera not function at all, but never just a visual anomaly in a recorded clip without other interruption. What really gives me pause about this moment is its timing. The shadow coincided precisely with my having a strong enough physical reaction that I felt I needed to leave. The moment the shadow fills my car is the moment I started to feel unwell. In all honesty, all things considered, it feels like the spirits were a little tired of my presence and were sending a message that it was time to go. I'm glad I took the hint, albeit unconsciously. I'm realizing that not every cemetery is alike. Some feel peaceful and inviting, some continue to make me feel unwelcome. So, though I am more open-minded about cemetery visits these days, I think I'm still finding my way with them. But now, I let myself stand in my discomfort in burial spaces as one would stand in chilly pool water, letting myself adjust until I feel comfortable enough to continue. I have not run.

As I've gotten deeper and deeper into the paranormal

community, I have befriended morticians, funeral directors, and even death doulas, all of whom have unknowingly helped me overcome a deep-seated automatic avoidance I have had around death, just through simple friendly, open conversation and their naturally empathetic reactions– something I lacked in my youth. Other paranormal investigators, unabashedly searching for ghosts with me in the dark, have helped me see death through the lens of compassion, normalcy, and inevitability. Each time I wrap up an interesting macabre conversation with a friend, or part ways in the morning after a late-night investigation, I feel a bit more healed, reminded again that I made the right choice in joining this field. I'd needed some guidance in my journey learning about death, and here it was, nestled in new friendships.

CHAPTER 44

THE PERILS & POSITIVES OF SOCIAL MEDIA

T hrough the years, some of my macabre explorations have been motivated by the desire to share my adventures with others online. While this may sound vapid or flimsy, it has actually been helpful in pushing me beyond my comfort zone and inspiring me to take action. Instead of sitting on the couch scrolling my phone, seeing others' adventures, or watching yet another repeat episode of a paranormal show, I'm throwing on my shoes and driving to some new location to see what it's like in person. With my responsibilities at home, I cannot always dedicate my weekends to full paranormal investigations, so my day trips have been crucial to satisfying my need for a spooky fix.

Some of my most interesting daytime excursions, often with my kids in tow, have been these oddball visits to haunted or creepy places I wanted to share on social media. While I maintain that I don't think all paranormal experiences are meant to be shared, posting short videos and explanations of interesting local spots to explore has enriched my days. I have been inspired by others who go on similar ventures, and I try to add to the veritable catalog myself as I go. In sharing my adventures via social media, I have met other like-minded people and content creators who also visit strange and obscure places, or who want to discuss my experiences. I've found a weird little community for my weird little self, and though it certainly has its downfalls, finding compatible friends through social media has been fun and profoundly validating.

To successfully pull yourself out from any dark period in your life, you must find community, whether you like it or not. I'd say I have always been a loner and homebody by nature, but no woman is an island, and even us introverts need a listening ear from time to time. I'm lucky to have a few steadfast pillars of support in my life – a loving husband, a handful of friends who truly understand me, some family, but when engaging in a new hobby as part of your mental health "therapy," so to speak, finding the correlating community helps your passion bloom. When I started, no one in my social circle was a paranormal nerd like myself, I found the paranormal community online, and I'm continually amazed by their creativity, open minds, and adventurous spirits. I've found that while, oddly, I don't mind public speaking so much, I tend to be an introvert one-on-one, often second-guessing all the weird responses coming out of my mouth or overthinking everything afterward. Online, it is much easier to explore my expressive freedom and be spontaneous. I love creating videos, posts, and text to share my ideas. Adding my voice to the throng of other weird perspectives is liberating and something I might not always have the confidence to do in an in-person setting. Not yet, anyway. It has occasionally been the case that I met a new friend by connecting through one single photo and caption I'd dithered on sharing. I joke that I'm always potentially one post away from a new weird friend.

In this day of social media and instant information sharing,

I've noticed a dichotomy of individuals who "hunt ghosts." There are those who team up with people from their region, geographically speaking, and there are those who take to the internet to connect with people of similar interests across the globe. I have dabbled in a little bit of both and found real connections with people in both local and online communities. In the end, what's truly important in friendship, regardless of where they live and how you connect, is respect, common values, laughter, and trust.

In seeking friendship, I gravitate toward women who truly build each other up and cheer for each other's success. I'm not necessarily looking for such things as "follower count" or "aesthetic" in a friend, though it has been far too easy to slide into caring too much about these trivial factors and miss the individual behind the screen. These days, it's easy to see huge follower numbers and make all kinds of assumptions. People typically put their best foot forward online – essentially a curated album of their life's highlight reel as their internet persona. I think most of us are guilty of this; even as I seek to connect with people, I hold them at arm's length until I'm comfortable. (The depths of my weirdness and my bad jokes are a prize only for those poor souls who truly befriend me.) In the end, real connection with another person has very little to do with their outward online presence; it's merely a place to start getting to know them, whether they have thousands of followers or a hundred.

I have been so lucky to transform some online friends into in-person friends over the years. We've driven hours and hours up and down the East Coast to meet up and spend time together, investigating spooky spots, of course, but also just talking, laughing, and sharing meals together. I leave these too-few-and-far-between weekends with that precious bubble of connection within me. There are still more friends who I have yet to meet face-to-face, but I value our endless streams of messages each day. Few people will take a deep dive into the topic of egregores with you; I hold on tight to them when I find them. Meeting these people in the world brings with it validation in my choice to embrace my weirdness, and of my capacity to contribute as an adult and not "just a mother." That human-to-human connection, based on a common interest in spooky things, was another piece of what gradually pulled me from my stagnant haze of the day-to-day grind. There's a quote from famed *Narnia* author C. S. Lewis that encapsulates it perfectly:

"Friendship... is born at the moment when one man says to another, "What! You too? I thought that no one but myself..."[62]

As in any social sphere, finding your people takes some work. Inevitably, you encounter some bumps along the way. Sometimes a bump leaves a bruise.

After a few years of navigating the paranormal "social scene," so to speak, I've found that it holds the same potential for social strife as any other community, unfortunately. I fancy myself old enough to dodge a lot of unnecessary tension, but I suppose it's just a part of life, especially in these days spent online. As much as I'd love to say I've been unbothered and my path to finding my tribe was easy, acidic input from strangers readily lobbed through the internet is a bummer, and all too common. I am tougher than I was when I first began my public paranormal journey, but I'm a normal person with a fair amount of emotional baggage, and sometimes someone's comments will hit you right in the feels.

One memorable instance early on in joining the community serves as a cautionary tale worthy of sharing. A few months into joining the *paracommunity*, as it's sometimes called, I received a private message from an online acquaintance to randomly let me know that her *psychic* perception of me was that I was hyper and chaotic. She went on to tell me I was inauthentic, and I needed to do a better job of acknowledging my dark side, to do more "shadow work" to connect more deeply with the dark parts of myself and the field, because I seemed "afraid, both figuratively and in reality." I was taken aback both by her assessment of me and her desire to tell me all of this, and I responded to her to say so. She replied that she was trying to help me "shape my content." It had been over a decade since I graduated high school, yet here I was again; I know a veiled insult when I see one. I was new to sharing so openly and already feeling fragile, but I'd been staying in my lane, and sharing my paranormal journey had been fun and therapeutic so far. I don't mind constructive criticism, but this wasn't what this was.

Now, goodness knows women get enough constant critique in this world, so you'd think maybe these comments rolled off my back and I thought nothing of them, but this person's words hurt and angered me. They blindsided me and made me question everything I'd openly shared with this new community, which had been difficult to do in the first place. I felt stupid; I wanted to pull it all back in somehow. She was partially right; I definitely *was* afraid of some things I was trying to work through, but I hadn't pretended false bravado. I was embarrassed to be called hyper, as a thirty-seven-year-old mother (who is extremely organized, by the way), and I was irritated to feel the need to defend myself. To be so bluntly insulted under the guise of helpfulness was the least helpful behavior I could have encountered. And to have it come from someone I admired at the time, who consistently posted about feminism and lifting each other up, made me question the quality of what (and where) I was sharing, and whether I had the right to join in at all. I felt very disillusioned and less positive about the community in which I now was growing tentative friendships, and I nearly stopped entirely. This feeling is why I feel compelled to share this particular interaction, trite though it may sound. A relative stranger had made me feel unsafe and ashamed, when in reality, I had been making great personal progress.

I took a breather and remembered the reasons why being in this community mattered to me, and why I joined the field at all. My "why" was bigger than anyone could tell from a handful of social media posts. As I was mulling it over, I had a "Robin Williams in *Good Will Hunting*" moment and felt some peace as I remembered something: I'd pulled myself out from the well. I'd been to the dark places in my mind and worked to climb out and away from them. I may not always share my private experiences – that is until I sit and spend a year writing a book about them – but for someone ten plus years my junior to offer unsolicited advice telling me to work on myself ended up telling me more about her than myself. She was seeing me through her lens.

As this type of online bullying (thinly disguised as help or not) is an unfortunate part of our lives these days, it deserves to be acknowledged, even if it seems silly to mention. Online bullying is all too real. It's difficult in the moment but shouldn't dissuade anyone from following their passions. In the end, it was a reminder to keep my guard up a bit more and choose my crowd more carefully. I didn't enter into some inane internet comment war, but it stays tucked away in my memory, a red flag if there ever was one. Happily, for every negative interaction, of which there have been very few, there are a dozen positive ones. Every day I give and receive supportive comments, partake in interesting conversations, and laugh out loud over hilarious messages sent my way by those who have come to know me. I have friends in the field who know I'm sharing what I've experienced in a truthful and authentic way. I'm not for everyone; no one is. I've continued to share what I want to share, how I want to share it, and I've found a niche that fits. What's the point otherwise?

Sometimes it's prudent to take a moment to reflect on your strength and protect your personal energy. We do not owe the world our private thoughts for consumption, despite what seems to be expected of us these days. My perspective as an investigator, relatively new to the scene compared to some, means I'm coming in with fresh eyes and my own point of view. We all have that right. Freedom of expression is important; I can post optimistic and bright moments on my paranormal platform while still taking the field seriously. To embrace color and joy and the full range of human emotion is to show due respect to paranormal research; it is not necessarily shying away from the darkness. We're sharing how our research about ghosts makes us feel. Yes, we are spending time in dark, spooky places, but if there are ghosts in the shadows, they were likely people once too, with the range of emotions we have now. A lesson from this Mom: do not mistake brightness for weakness.

In addition to these types of mundane little social clashes that inevitably pop up anytime people interact, it's worth acknowledging that I have indeed found a bit of other unpleasant issues I'd been cautioned about when I first started sharing my adventures. The more I embraced the paranormal field and waded in, the more there was. It could eat you up if you let it – the pressure of scheduling the next event, the narcissism of posting content online, and just being a woman in the paranormal can be unsurprisingly difficult. It's easy to focus too much on the endless data available at your fingertips – a quantification of how much the online world "values" you. While it has been an overall positive addition to my life when I needed a way to reach out, it also brought along these new complications I've had to work my way through. The straight truth is that I cannot say yes to every travel invitation extended to me, as much as I might want to. I have responsibilities in my home, raising my children and tending to my adult life, and those have to come first, no matter how you slice it. I don't resent that, but I do resent that sometimes I'm sure I come across as disinterested or undedicated. I've needed to remind myself not to compare my relative value and contributions to those of others, nor seek external validation in my journey.

Despite some hiccups navigating social media, it has yielded some fun opportunities I wouldn't have had without it, in addition to valued friendships. I was published twice in a project spearheaded by a friend I met online – a women's journal of the strange and unusual. I became a contributor on two online dark tourism blogs and felt bold enough to submit writing elsewhere. I've met and befriended paranormal personalities I'd watched on television for years. I've been invited as a guest to chat on various podcasts and internet shows, and made friends around the world I never would have met otherwise. For one extraordinary week, I was even briefly considered to be on a nationwide competition show on network television after they found my account online – I didn't make it past the first casting call, but I still enjoy the memory. All in all, social media is tricky territory; it's a path to some exciting prospects, especially in the paranormal field, but there are plenty of pitfalls to avoid along the way. However, if you can navigate it while maintaining your integrity and your "why," despite how many followers you do or do not have, it's a wonderful tool to dive into community.

Time and again, I find contentment when I remind myself of my reasons for beginning. When I'm knee-deep in laundry and my world is starting to feel small, I think back over all the strange experiences I've had. I think of the history I've learned about and the places I've explored firsthand, and I feel refreshed. I love the thrill of being in on the action in-person and seeing these strangely beautiful places with my own eyes. I have found that every investigation leaves its mark on me – not literally, thank goodness, but I learn something new everywhere I go. I cherish the friends I've made and the conversations we've had. Each experience I have hones the set of paranormal parameters I walk around with, and every rabbit hole seems to hold ten more rabbit holes inside it. I am constantly scrambling to draw up definitions of what I believe, a reminder again and again of just how damn big and interesting the world is. Sounds like a pretty good "why" to me.

PART FOUR

LESSONS FROM GHOSTS

CHAPTER 45

LESSONS FROM GHOSTS

The significance of welcoming the paranormal into my life has not been from some massive TV-documentary-worthy experience in which an entity followed me home and wreaked havoc upon my life. I haven't solved the decades-long mystery of an unknown spirit's identity nor captured undeniable video evidence of the afterlife. What I have found is my own unexplainable experiences, and my embracing the search has improved the quality of my time and made me recognize hidden parts of myself. My journey is rather far more relatable to the typical experience of the amateur "ghost hunter": investigating hauntings as much as possible, researching historical ties and strange theories, and finding community with others in the field. I'm excited that I've merely laid the groundwork for bigger, bolder, and scarier adventures ahead.

Why has the paranormal helped me through the stresses from the demands of motherhood and in turn helped me fully appreciate it? How has my perspective changed since I started investigating haunted locations?

It's still a work in progress. *I'm* still a work in progress. I've learned to balance my subjective inklings with objective reasoning. I realized that I can be comfortable with not always reaching a definitive explanation, something I thought would forever bother me. What I truly know is that I've felt and seen things, both in the paranormal sense and in terms of my own potential, that are radically different from what I once believed. Most importantly, I've pushed myself to be braver, bolder, and more adventurous than I thought I ever could be. And looking back on it all, there are a few key pieces of the big picture that have shifted for me, and I'm sure there will be more as I continue on the path ahead.

THERE IS SUCH A THING AS GHOSTS

There's a statement I wouldn't have uttered publicly before this journey, but here we are. Ghosts exist, and paranormal experiences aren't *always* the fabrication of the individual telling their story. I don't feel the need to prove my opinion to those who think otherwise; it's just something I now know and accept. And maybe that makes me weird, but if you haven't been paying attention thus far – I'm ok with that.

Knowing ghosts exist, that they can sometimes interact with our plane of existence, still blows my mind, and that belief alone fractures into questions about so many experiences in my life. In a broader, almost overwhelming sense, it makes me take a different view on who we are as a species, and all the different belief systems in the world. If part of our selves remains intact posthumously, then what happens after death? Is there something we do in life to give us ghostly form in the hereafter? Does knowing ghosts exist prompt any changes in the way I live my life, or should it? It hasn't yet; I wouldn't even know what to start or stop doing that would affect the outcome. Part of me doubts that it is up to us one way or the other.

Truly believing in ghosts is simultaneously frightening and comforting to me. As much as I hate to think of any soul left waiting around on Earth in some ethereal stasis, I now wonder at all those moments in life when I felt the energy of my grandmother's presence near me, as if checking in on me. Perhaps that was real. But does that mean she isn't resting in peace? Can spirits choose to visit us and then return to a place of rest? These are the rabbit-hole thought spirals that keep a paranormal investigator booking event after event, hoping for another glimpse behind the curtain, something else that either fits or dismisses a theory, or just lets them sleep at night.

GHOSTS AREN'T NECESSARILY WHAT WE'VE ALWAYS THOUGHT THEM TO BE

I think a part of me always knew ghosts were real; the confirmation was a bonus. The question of *what* they are is a paranormal topic that both thrills and confounds me – the possibilities surrounding the conversation are fascinating. I think most paranormal investigators and enthusiasts have tried to answer this question at some point, if only privately. I believe there are different types of spiritual energies that we interpret as ghosts.

Some ghosts are the classic, Halloween-esque belief of what ghosts are – spirits from individuals who have yet to move on, stuck in some sort of purgatory on Earth after death has claimed their physical body. I am referring here to the "intelligent spirit," a ghost who can respond and react, who has some way to actively communicate and make itself known. In some cases, it really is the scenario of "unfinished business" keeping them rooted to their earthly life's story. For others, it may be a love for a house or location that keeps them tethered. For others, it might be trauma or a tragedy at death that keeps them. A large part of me hopes that these types of spirits can come and go from this plane; it's a dreadful thought for any soul to be "stuck."

Some ghosts are echoes of emotions or traumatic events, the oft-referred-to "residual spirit," collected in a location or object, as described in Stone Tape theory. Under the heading of this classification of ghost is the entity, or a partial entity, that follows the same path or action on repeat without acknowledging others. These types of spirits do not have the capacity to interact – if you experience one, it is like witnessing a moment in time, not a sentient remaining soul. For example, I believe the full-body apparition I witnessed at the Shanley Hotel was a residual spirit – perhaps a lady of the night or the madam of the brothel making her usual brisk rounds, crossing that hallway without a moment of thought cast in our direction. Sometimes, a residual spirit manifests as a strong echo of an emotion or a palpable feeling in an environment – not a discernible being at all. Some paranormal theorists will include time slip phenomena under the umbrella of "residual spirit," though I think that branch of classification has its own unique defining qualities, and personally I think a ghost seen in a time slip scenario can potentially be intelligent.

For those who believe in time slips, some paranormal experiences or ghost sightings may indicate such a moment. Where a fold in the so-called time fabric exists, where the ever-undulating timeline might overlap, however briefly, we can experience the unexpected. Some investigators recall hearing their own voices calling out to them, and wonder if it is their younger or older selves visiting the same location at a different point in their lives. Much like the ideas of an egregore or poltergeist activity, this view on ghosts suggests that investigators themselves may affect the environment. Are we generating our own ghosts; are we haunting ourselves?

If the ideas of time slip hauntings and egregores aren't enough, there are other belief systems assuming ghosts (and even cryptids like Bigfoot) are glimpses of parallel dimensions or demons, fae, inhuman entities, and even aliens. I acknowledge and will listen to just about any paranormal theory, but bringing aliens into the mix is a whole separate ballgame right there. What I have covered is merely the tip of a fascinating and strange iceberg. Feel free to begin your research by typing any of this into your internet search engine. I promised rabbit holes, and rabbit holes you shall have.

WHETHER OR NOT YOU EXPERIENCE GHOSTLY ACTIVITY MIGHT BE PARTLY UP TO YOU

I saw that full-body apparition in the spring of 2021, and my life view was forever altered. Would I have seen that ghost if I had been sitting in a corner seat of the room, churlish and openly mocking the entire evening's activities? I don't know. Apart from ruining the group dynamic acting like that, a spirit may not be able to connect through that kind of energetic interference. For better or for worse, your openness and mental state may affect whether or not you see, hear, or feel the paranormal. (This is not in reference to nor mocking mental illness or medication-induced hallucinations.)

There are tales of a diehard skeptic having a paranormal experience that changed his or her views, but do you need to *want* to see a ghost, on some level? I have found time and again that my mood and relative "openness" at an investigation or a spooky location affects what I experience. If I have an argument before an investigation, or even if I'm engaged in a conversation heavy with complaints or negativity while en route to a location, the night ahead falls flat. Perhaps I'd be quicker to dismiss an experience while in a foul mood. Or maybe going in distracted, I simply miss attempts at spiritual engagement, the negativity having changed my energy so much that I wasn't able to tune in at all. Would you want to speak to someone so obviously grouchy? To combat this mental and emotional interference, it can be helpful to engage in simple grounding practices leading up to an event. Really, grounding can be helpful any day of the week to start fresh and neutral for what each day has in store.

I'm not a huge fan of yoga or burning sage bundles, but grounding doesn't necessarily have to follow any New Age rules or expectations, unless that works for you. What matters is that your grounding process fits you, with the intention of feeling calmer and more resilient afterward. The average non-paranormally-inclined mom would tuck grounding activities under the "self-care" umbrella. Some use crystals or medita-tion; some swear off social media for a few days. Personally, when I'm trying to center my mind, I try to cut way back on social media consumption and spend more present time with my family. I like to burn a favorite palo santo candle and try to take a few moments of mindful gratitude. Whatever the method, in the paranormal, grounding is meant to help you go into a haunted location protected but open to activity. A neutral-to-positive attitude coupled with respectful intent is like a blank canvas for fantastic experiences.

If you feel like you can ground yourself but still haven't experienced much, or you long to *see* a spirit even though you occasionally hear a disembodied voice, there's good news, so to speak. Another factor in whether or not you might experi-ence something paranormal might be partially up to your intu-itive senses and perceptive skills. Some people are gifted with extraordinary perceptive powers – the "clair-" senses discussed previously. Different people can experience the same haunting differently. Sometimes everyone in the room will hear the same odd sound or see the same unexplained light, but sometimes, two people standing next to each other will have completely different experiences.

I believe deep immersion into paranormal study and investigations can develop your "clair-" senses and observation skills. Like learning on the job, the further you go into researching and seeking out paranormal experiences, the finer your perceptive skills get. You can hone them as you gain experience. A practiced eye might dismiss a shadow from a nearby tree when you may have once thought it to be a shadow person. Your intuitive senses may naturally get stronger the more you use them, as a muscle gains strength with exercise. I think this learning can be intentional or coincidental, as I have never tried to learn how to see spirits, yet, one day, I did. I will never be one of those people who walks into a room full of investigators to boldly declare that I self-identify as a clairaudient or clairvoyant, but I have heard and seen unexplainable things, so maybe I have inadvertently developed those skills along the way.

If all else fails, ditch all your recording equipment, sit alone in the creepiest room of the next haunted location you visit, and test my theory that spirits will interact the most when you're not trying to capture the moment. I triple dog dare you. (For the record, that's a dare I might not even accept myself, some nights.)

PARANORMAL INVESTIGATING ISN'T ONLY ABOUT THE GHOSTS

From my perspective, paranormal investigation has been some weird form of pseudo-therapy – a new source of inspiration, and a wild hobby to shake up everyday life. When I look back on my time as a paranormal investigator, I see now that it's not always about what spooky evidence I've captured; those bits of audio and video aren't necessarily always my favorite memories from overnights. Paranormal investigations are about the people around you as much as they're about the ghosts you seek. There's no denying that sitting in the dark, talking to nothing is a weird way to spend your time. I think back on all the friends I've made, and all the odd experiences that have bonded us. The friendships you make while discussing and investigating the paranormal are unlike any others you will make in life. If you are lucky enough to find others you can trust enough to explore these old, creepy locations with, and make jokes with, and get really deep in the Weird with, you are very lucky indeed.

PEACE IS WORTH IT

I read an anonymous quote recently that struck me so acutely:

"Each morning, peace arrives at your door in the form of choices."

Making difficult, sometimes weird decisions about how you live your life, based on what will bring you the most peace, is transformative. I've made decisions, tried things, and embraced ideas that are way off the beaten path, but that align with my truth. I was scared, nervous, and sometimes unsure whether to proceed with these decisions, but living my life fully in this way has helped me blossom. I looked into myself and tried to locate what would truly make me full of the joy of life. What was I missing? The answer to that won't look the same for everyone, even to others in the paranormal field. I've taken chances I had to psych myself up for: I've held my breath and sent an email or dialed a phone number, eager for a response. Not everything has come to fruition, and not every opportunity came my way. But the ones that have are some of my most cherished experiences, and I'm still proud of trying for the ones that didn't pan out. When I've reached outside my comfort zone, I've enjoyed some experiences that years ago, I never would have dreamed possible. While the first steps were anything but peaceful sometimes, the end result of letting myself try new things has always felt like a deep breath of cool autumn air.

Your choices don't always need to be shouted from the rooftops or in a tweet – you can just quietly make the choice and keep moving forward toward your peace. You can share as much or as little of yourself as you want; you are not obligated to share your energy. Some people in your life or across the internet may not understand or support your new, bold, or unusual choices – that's ok. You are the heroine of your story. If your choices come from a thoughtful place of aligning your actions with what you truly want, things will fall in line. It might be a bumpy road to get there, but reaching your version of peace is a goal that is worth a rough patch of transition. I speak from experience, while I continue to make new weird choices, seemingly on a daily basis.

LEAN INTO THE WEIRD PARTS OF YOURSELF

This is the most profound conclusion I have drawn from my experiences over the past few years, and it bleeds into other lessons I've learned. Sometimes finding peace will mean you need to drop that curtain behind which you are hiding yourself. For me, paranormal investigation is bigger than the activity itself – it's about being proud to try something that a lot of people are flat-out too judgmental or too scared to try. I see a dark and crumbling hallway, and my instinct is to walk down it, hoping to see or hear something unexplainable, while most would run the other way. It makes me feel like some cool badass Final Girl; it's a little fire I carry with me when I come home and make flyers for my kid's elementary school fundraiser the next day. "I'm a badass," I whisper to myself as I click the Print button.

For any person feeling hollow, directionless, unfulfilled – there is always an answer. Throughout my life, trying new things or going after ideas that sparked excitement within me have time and again helped fight off waves of darkness threatening to swallow me up. Everyone has had a moment of shoving aside those parts of themselves that are "weird" or embarrassing. But those who don't acknowledge them are missing out. Though I enjoy my "mainstream" interests – reading, cooking, etc. – nothing makes me feel more unique or more excited than paranormal investigating. It's the field and friends I've made, yes, but it is also coming to terms with accepting all of myself, like a lesson from some Disney movie.

My weird parts are some of the most fun parts and are the ones that help me feel like I have a unique perspective in this world. Life is too damn short to spend it not doing what you want to do, even if it can only be feasibly done in short bursts here and there around your larger responsibilities.

The sentiment of self-reflection and questioning your life path is not only a message for burnt-out mothers. I am no professional – therapist or ghost hunter – but I am a mother, and Mom is telling you: there is always, always hope, and it is never too late. It's never too late to try something new or dive into something unusual. It may not be paranormal investigating, though if you have considered it, I highly recommend trying it at least once. You can begin by visiting any of the incredible locations I've mentioned, or find a public hunt at a haunted location near you. It's a quick search of social media to find a local paranormal group where you live. We're everywhere. The odds are nothing will happen your first time out, but it may ensnare you anyway. And if something incredible does occur, if there's one little unexplainable moment that sticks with you, you may be hooked. Either way, you'll have gone out on a limb, met some new people, and likely impressed yourself with your own bravery, and that's the win. Get uncomfortable in a good way. Grow. Find your Weird.

FINAL THOUGHTS,
FOR NOW

Is trying new things, especially unusual ones, nerve-racking? Yes. Is researching the paranormal, "hunting for ghosts," scary? Absolutely. But real fears are the ones that go deep. They're the ones that keep you up at night, circling around and around, keeping you from blessed sleep. When it comes right down to it, identifying your fears is important; they show you what matters.

What keeps me up until the hours when my eyes are dry and longing to close? What comes to mind when I am comfortable in my bed, but my brain is rifling through scenarios that send a chill down my spine, prompting me to form plans against it? For me, my biggest fear isn't the ghosts I've encountered. It is and always has been that my children will one day decide I failed them in some core moments of their lives, so much so that a rift must exist between us for them to feel peace. I'm determined to beat this particular fear. I'm determined to be happier, brighter, and optimistic for them. I try to keep balance between their needs and my own, without tipping the scale too far in either direction. It's a difficult tightrope; it's work.

I do still sometimes have a handful of days where I mess up, or where I feel so blue I'm numb. It happens. But I've learned to take it easier on myself those days, and I know now that not every low period means I'm headed for catastrophe. I have a network of valued friends and family, my health, and compelling interests to keep me afloat long enough to send my blues running. The work I've put into boldly being myself has been worth it. I'm very grateful for that. While I know full well it's not so simple for everyone, I do think readying a net of passionate interests is beneficial for everyone. Maybe one day they'll help catch you as you fall.

When it comes to healing old wounds (the "ghosts" of my past, if you will), particularly with my mother, compassion on my part is a constant struggle. It's not my favorite thing about myself. The mother-daughter bond is a sacred relationship, but I've swallowed a bitter pill about some aspects of how I was raised; some parts of me feel permanently iced over in self-preservation. It is difficult to thaw and might not even be in anyone's best interest at this point; it's hard to say. Some might say I need to prioritize making amends; I have tried many times and felt the pain of crushed hope as many times. As a mother myself, now I can look back at her actions and differentiate somewhat between struggles that all mothers face versus choices she made while suffering from serious mental health issues. I love my mom. She's not a villain; she never has been. She's been sick a long time. She didn't have the network of friends, family, and invested passions I fought to develop, but she didn't try to remedy that either. In her defense, I truly don't think she comprehends the impact of my early childhood on my life as it is now, nor the many painful moments we've shared through the years since. We had our good moments, our great moments. I still feel the urge to call her when *The Mummy* starring Brendan Fraser is on TV, or when I pull out old Halloween decorations that remind me of her. I acknowledge that she's clearly had a lot of pain over the span of most of her life; I just wish she'd tried harder to find her own peace, both selfishly, and for her own wellness. So, while my goal is to hold a neutral space so my kids can know her, I maintain my boundaries, and it is often difficult for me to let her in. My hide has been toughened after so many years. I draw a hard line if I think my children may end up in the line of emotional fire.

I'm doing the work I wish my own mother had done, to make sure I'm still a person while my children are becoming their own people. It's a fine balance between shifting my attention to and fro, but I think if it can be accomplished, I will set my children up for an emotionally healthy adulthood, where I am their rock. Most importantly, I openly and calmly try to answer my children's questions as openly and honestly as I can. More often than not these days, their queries involve requests for Pokémon cards or candy, but I don't shy away from the "tough" topics when they do come up. I show them it's ok to be sad or angry, or both, and that it's important to be grateful for our time and for each other. While I might not have a textbook-perfect answer every time, I won't ignore their curious minds and change the subject to easier ground. I can hold their hands as they find their ways, with the big topics, the small ones, and all the medium ones in between. It's part of the job. Yes, my children will have memories of me being angry (kids sure know how to push buttons) and sad (hello, I'm human), but I hope mostly they will remember me from their early years in a positive light, laughing and excited about new ideas and weird concepts. My dream is that when my children are adults, we can all joyfully sit together to chat about our interests around the dinner table. "Remember when Mom said she saw that ghost at the Shanley Hotel? What a weirdo!" I can see it already.

Somehow, this paranormal world fills a void I was developing. It is something so separate from how I spend the rest of my waking hours, something paramount for any mother. When I was feeling hollow and burned out, beat up after years of finding temporary fixes to get me through, I turned to paranormal research, of all things, and found something special. I figuratively said my "what the hell?" to the ether and jumped in. I transformed my interest from watching from the sidelines into being an active player on the field, and it's awakened some brave part of me who doesn't mind a small scare to find evidence of what may lie beyond.

I have noticed, if I do feel comfortable sharing with others outside the field (the "normies" as I call them) that I investigate haunted places, the response I get is typically one of fascination, coupled with a quirk of an eyebrow. Sometimes it's followed by their sharing a ghost story of their own. I don't automatically share this part of myself with everyone I come across, and yes, I often get bizarre looks and the tight-lipped expressions of a skeptic holding back a smug comment. Those reactions don't bother me. I take pride in the fact that I walk calmly into the dark and search for evidence of spirits who want to be heard. Many other mothers I know have asked if they can join me on an investigation, once they can talk themselves into getting over the fear of it, and I want them to. Investigations offer a liberating and strange sort of exhilaration, shaking loose the cobwebs of daily life. I think they can sense the thrill of adventure waiting on the other side of bravery.

I find myself unconsciously speaking to fellow mothers when I write; I'm passionate about sharing my unusual journey, even while it's still in progress. But to any soul feeling "stuck," mother or not, young or old, woman or man: I hope my words of my self-discovery inspire you. If you are feeling like your shine has been dulled by the weight of the world, I write to you. It doesn't have to be paranormal research that shakes things up in your life. It's just about looking inside and finding that strange bright thread that is wound through you. Grasp on and follow it until you feel that frisson of a thrill... then follow it further.

Self-care, in even its strangest forms, is crucial as we move forward on this plane. Reaching for small pieces of the big paranormal puzzle has enriched my life in so many ways, and I'm so pleased I was bold enough to embrace this part of myself. I have had not only ghostly experiences I had only ever dreamed of experiencing myself, but unique opportunities. It's offered more than a mere distraction to get me through a rough patch; it's become a piece of what defines me.

The discovery of an entire community of like-minded weirdos who made me feel accepted and encouraged has been invaluable. The connections I've made through this community and our shared ideas, from egregores to poltergeists and more, have awakened me from the motherhood catatonia into which I was slipping. Sharing my experiences on social media and with friends has helped me come into myself somehow. In turn, it's helped me embrace my time with my children, as can only happen when you are feeling fulfilled as a whole and not resentful. You cannot pour from an empty cup, and your children shouldn't be your only identity. I want to be the mother who has ideas to share and a contagious zest for life. I can always feel the original excitement about paranormal research when I touch base with my "why." Only then do I feel the peace that first came with jumping into this hobby.

I don't know if it's possible to ever finish processing one's ideas on the paranormal. Like parenthood, in those moments when you see your child succeed and feel your heart swell with love and pride, you wonder what's next; what more could possibly be in store on this amazing, wild ride? On each path, in the paranormal and in raising our children, we find more, experience more, and feel the thrill of expanding our minds to wrap around new ideas of what is possible in this world. Each is a never-ending adventure that keeps us finding new ideas and feelings, and then the next, and the next. And maybe that constant pull to seek out and discover new adventures is the entire point. Of paranormal investigating. Of parenting. Of it all.

AFTERWORD

As I was outlining ideas for this book/essay/embarrassingly long diary entry, I kept returning to the idea of pursuing weird hobbies as self-care. Motherhood is hard – it's the hardest twenty-four-seven job on the planet, and we mothers have got to start taking better care of ourselves. I don't care how you fill your cup up, but you need to. If paranormal investigation is your ticket – great, please find me on social media channels because we are officially new best friends. If it's something else – anything else – competitive quilting, beekeeping – go for it, and then find me on social media anyway, because I want to cheer for you.

And a love letter to my children, should they ever read their mother's words and worry that I ever regretted becoming a mother, let me be very clear: not for one second. My beautiful, kind, loving, hilarious, creative, smart, feisty kids: you are the best adventure I've ever had. No dark period in my life was ever your fault, and you are the best thing about me. Our family is a strong unit; the most important thing to me is to give you a safe home base from which to fly into the world. I hope one day you'll come on a ghost hunt with your "weird" mom, but if not, that's ok too. You will find your own weird adventures – and I will cheer you along with every step, as always.

I had a difficult time deciding how much of my trauma to share. Given some horrible family situations others have endured and overcome, I hesitated to even call it trauma, though I suspect I was trying to minimize it, in a way. I tested a version of telling my story in which I cut out all references to my mother's mental health struggles, particularly her suicidal ideation, which understandably, she was not wild about my sharing openly. But that tidied up version wasn't real, it wasn't honest, and I've had enough of holding it in. I had dreaded the idea of being so vulnerable; I still didn't want to contribute to her seemingly endless mental anguish. In the end, recounting and sharing some of these moments (but not nearly all of them) has been a therapeutic process for me, but a part of me still, *still* carries that responsibility of carrying the load of her mental health. Old patterns are hard to break. I still feel responsible, and maybe with this I finally am a bit to blame. But at the same time, I've been emotionally battered and scarred, on repeat, and I decided to allow myself to tell my story. And if I would have hidden the complete picture, of either my childhood or my postpartum battle for my own mental health, I may have been withholding a moment that a reader needed to see. Some moment of familiarity that helps someone with a similar backstory or the same struggles with parenthood feel a little less alone. That was worth it to me.

In writing this, I found myself forcing connections between each of my paranormal investigation stories with a facet of my motherhood journey. Sometimes the connections felt so intrinsic, wrapped up in my identity in general, it was sometimes hard to articulate. Some experiences and the impact they have had on me are clearly related to my struggles as a mother – I could see parallels, for example, in a paranormal lesson of grounding before being open and present, or even finding my maternal nature helpful in an investigation situation, as in talking to a child ghost. But there are many experiences that have nothing to do with my being a mother whatsoever.

But perhaps that is exactly *why* some of my paranormal study has been so important to me – not just in finding community on social media or forming friendships with individuals I'd only seen on TV through the years – but the very fact that I cannot always easily connect my paranormal experiences to my being a mother. They can be wholly separate, and that in itself is special to me.

Not every part of yourself has to be connected to your motherhood. You are more than a mom. These days, it is all too easy to absolutely lose ourselves in the mandatory sacrifices we make and the generalized anonymity of "Mom." And I declare this from a place of love – my children are the dearest souls on the Earth to me. But to help them better, to be their rock, to show them a model of resiliency – I need to step into myself fully. I need to engage weird, scary, sometimes embarrassingly unusual parts of what makes me, me so that I can help them do the same. My being comfortable with my weirdness will hopefully be a model for them to accept the weird quirks of themselves – we all have a few... some more than others.

I have this quote from *The Minds Journal* photoshopped over a photo of myself at my first investigation, exploring Fort Mifflin, on the night I heard my first disembodied voice:

"The shit that makes your heart beat faster and your eyes glow when you do it or talk about it, no matter if it's hiking, yoga, sex, gardening... do that. Do it as often as you can. Because that's what life's about. Creating as many passionate, happy moments as possible. Don't let anyone stop you from doing the things you love – not even yourself."

PHOTOS

Outside Selma Mansion, Norristown, PA, June 2022

My children at Selma Mansion, Norristown, PA, September
2021

Investigating Pennhurst State School, Spring City, PA, July
2020

The Catacombs at Bube's Brewery, Mount Joy, PA, October 2020

The Shanley Hotel, Napanoch, NY, March 2021

*View down the hallway inside the Shanley Hotel where I saw a
full-body apparition, Napanoch, NY, March 2021*

*My son at the Pawling Sycamore Witness Tree, Valley Forge,
PA, August 2022*

Visiting Robert the Doll at the East Martello Museum, Key West,
FL, September 2020

Henry Mercer's Study in Fonthill Castle, Doylestown, PA,
December 2021

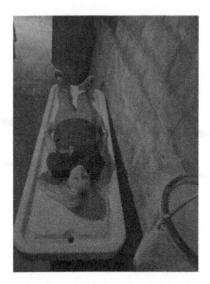

*Testing out the embalming table at the Wildwood Sanitarium,
Salamanca, NY, March 2022*

*The haunted ladies' room at McCoole's Tavern, Quakertown,
PA, February 2022*

The Sun Inn, Bethlehem, PA, May 2022

*Washington Memorial Chapel, Valley Forge National Park,
Valley Forge, PA, June 2022*

Copy of The Restless Painting, *on display in an undisclosed location, Lake George, NY, June 2022*

Estes Session at the Hinsdale House, Hinsdale, NY, March 2022

At home on my thirty-eighth birthday, March 2022

ACKNOWLEDGMENTS

To the team at Beyond the Fray, especially G. Michael Hopf, thank you for the chance to share my voice. To L. Douglas Hogan, thank you for your patience and graphic design skills.

To my ghouls Hilary Opiel, Karly Latham, Amy Bennett, Courtney Eastman, Amanda Woomer, Beckie-Ann Galentine, and Lorien Jones, for all the things.

To my friends in the paracommunity who have been there for investigations, weird conversation, inspiration, support, and laughs: Dave Schrader, Katie Whipple-Spracklin, Kelly Miller, Brandon Schuster, Jodi Nettles, Russ Blackmore, Cherise Williams, and Celeste Mott.

To Suzie Garofalo, my ride or die: you are a bright light to all who know you.

To Meg Erickson, my cousin but essentially my sister, who talked ghost shit with me before anyone else, I send love every day.

To Pam and Tommy Van Scoy, Ed and Deb Cywinski, and Ray Cywinski, you stepped in and have been my family since day one. No words can express my thanks and love.

To my parents, I know it was difficult. I love you.

To Ben, thank you and I love you. Where in the world would I be without you? Don't answer that. Also, you smell. To Laura and the boys, Damn, you are all amazing. And so much cooler than I am or ever will be.

To my children, Cade and Maya, I hope you always know

how much I love and like you and how proud I am of you, for all the little and big things. I'll always have your back. H, K, HF, FB, TU, P.

To my husband, Ed, thank you for all the ways you show me your love and support every day. You've seen all sides of me (insert racy joke here) and show me you love it all. Skeptic though you may be, it's you I want to cuddle up with after a spooky night.

REFERENCES (& RESOURCES FOR YOUR INDEPENDENT RABBIT HOLE RESEARCH)

Note: When writing in the paranormal nonfiction genre, it is often difficult to accurately cite sources on legend, opinion, and theory.

My memories are imperfect but I have shared my experiences and information regarding individuals, locations, and history to the best of my knowledge and available resources

1. Holzer, Hans. "The Ship Chandler's Ghost." *The Ghost Hunter* (50th Anniversary Edition ed). Fall River Press, New York, NY, 2014, pp. 238–239.

2. *The History of Fort Mifflin.* (n.d.). Fort Mifflin on the Delaware. Retrieved March 12, 2022, from http://www.fortmif flin.us/the-history/

3. Tandy, V.; Lawrence, T. (1998, April). "The ghost in the machine" (PDF). *Journal of the Society for Psychical Research.* 62 (851): 360–364.

4. Baylis, J., & Ting, D. K. (2015, December 7). "Pareidolia and clinical reasoning: the pattern awakens." *Canadian Medical Association Journal*, 187(18), 1364–1364. https://doi.org/10.1503/cmaj.151079

5. Merriam-Webster. (n.d.). Apophenia. In *Merriam-Webster.com dictionary*. Retrieved September 15, 2022, from https://www.merriam-webster.com/dictionary/apophenia

6. *Norristown Preservation Society*. (n.d.). Retrieved October 16, 2020, from https://www.norristownpreservationsociety.org/

7. Heath, P. R. (2005). "A New Theory on Place Memory." *Australian Journal of Parapsychology*. 5(1):40–58.

8. McCue, P. (2002). "Theories of Haunting: A Critical Overview" *Journal of the Society for Psychical Research*. 661(866):1–21.

9. Danielson, Lindsey. (2014). "Using GIS to Analyze Relationships to Explore Paranormal Occurrences in the Continental United States." *Saint Mary's University of Minnesota University Central Services Press*. Winona, MN. Retrieved September 15, 2022, from http://www.gis.smumn.edu

10. "EVP Classification: Are Your Spirit Voices 'Class A?'" (n.d.). Higgypop Paranormal. Retrieved June 7, 2022, from https://www.higgypop.com/news/evp-classification/

11. Newkirk, Greg. (2019, January 24). "The Estes Method: How the Groundbreaking SB7 Spirit Box Experiment is Changing Paranormal Investigation." Week in Weird. Retrieved September 15, 2022, from http://weekinweird.com/2019/01/24/estes-method-sb7-spirit-box-experiment-paranormal-investigation/

12. Pietrangelo, A. (2019, March 29). "Why Do I Have a Bad Taste in My Mouth?" Healthline. Retrieved January 10, 2022, from https://www.healthline.com/health/bad-taste-in-mouth

13. Davis, F. (2021, May 20*).* "4 Main Types of Intuitive Abilities & How to Strengthen Them." Cosmic Cuts. Retrieved August 1, 2022, from https://cosmiccuts.com/blogs/healing-stones-blog/intuitive-abilities

14. "About Pennhurst State School and Hospital." (n.d.).

Pennhurst Memorial & Preservation Alliance. Retrieved May 15, 2022, from http://www.preservepennhurst.org/default.aspx?pg=36

15. Sutton, S. C. (2017, May). "PENNHURST: AN EXPLORATION OF EXHIBITION AND COLLECTION CARE INSIDE A HAUNTED ASYLUM" [MA Thesis]. Temple University.

16. Lintner, J. (2022, September 15). "Historic building, with connections to the Underground Railroad, had many occupants since 1804." Retrieved September 15, 2022, from https://www.columbiaspy.com/2018/03/historic-building-with-connections-to.html

17. "If These Walls Could Talk." (n.d.). The Haunted Shanley Hotel. Retrieved March 14, 2021, from https://thehauntedshanleyhotel.com/our-history/

18. [The History Underground]. (2021, May 23). "The Slaughter at Devil's Den (Gettysburg)" / *History Traveler* Episode 132 [Video]. YouTube. Retrieved November 9, 2020, from https://www.youtube.com/watch?v=nm4ejprFj3o

19. Davis, D., PhD, M. C., & White, K. D. (2015, April 20). *Fight Like the Devil: The First Day at Gettysburg, July 1, 1863 (Emerging Civil War Series)* (1st ed.). Savas Beatie.

20. "Devil's Den – Gettysburg, PA." (2013, July 22). Places of Geologic Significance on Waymarking.com. Retrieved October 12, 2022, from https://www.waymarking.com/waymarks/WMHM9C_Devils_Den_Gettysburg_PA

21. Schrader, David. [The Paranormal 60 with Dave Schrader]. (2022, February 8). *The Paranormal 60 with Dave Schrader* "Let the Spirits Speak with Nick Groff, Cherise Williams & More" [Video]. YouTube. Retrieved October 6, 2022, from https://www.youtube.com/watch?v=uJwT0GPNTB0

22. Davies, R. (2019, August 24). *Time-Slips: Journeys into the Past and the Future.* Independently published.

23. Price-Williams, B. (2021, March 11). "The Terrifying Tale

of Pennsylvania's Haunted Inn At Herr Ridge Will Give You Nightmares." OnlyInYourState. Retrieved December 6, 2021, from https://www.onlyinyourstate.com/pennsylvania/inn-herr-ridge-haunted-pa/

24. Brown, B. (2021, April 29). "This B&B in New Hope Hid Aaron Burr after His Famous Duel with Alexander Hamilton." Retrieved November 1, 2021, from https://www.visit buckscounty.com/blog/post/this-bb-in-new-hope-hid-aaron-burr-after-his-famous-duel-with-alexander-hamilton/

25. "HISTORY | Bube's Brewery." (n.d.). Retrieved October 6, 2022, from https://bubesbrewery.com/history/

26. Woomer, A. R. (2020, July 13). *The Spirit Guide: America's Haunted Breweries, Distilleries, and Wineries.* Spook-Eats.

27. Heaney, K. C. (2017, August 15). "History, Hauntings and Hootenanny." Susquehanna Style. Retrieved October 6, 2022, from https://susquehannastyle.com/food/eat-&-drink/history-hauntings-and-hootenanny/

28. Nicholas, C. (2017, January 22). "Hinsdale Haunting, Western New York's Greatest Historical Folly." Obscure Casebook. Retrieved September 15, 2022, from https://www.obscurecasebook.com/single-post/2014/05/01/frozen-river

29. Miller, C. M. (2009, August 25). *Echoes of a Haunting – Revisited.* Virtualbookworm.com Publishing.

30. Sparrow, M. (1976, October 6). *Conjuring up Philip: An Adventure In Psychokinesis* (1st US ed). Harper & Row.

31. Wehrstein, K. M. (n.d.). "Philip Psychokinesis Experiments." Psi Encyclopedia. Retrieved October 6, 2022, from https://psi-encyclopedia.spr.ac.uk/articles/philip-psychokinesis-experiments

32. Stavish, M. *Egregores: The Occult Entities That Watch Over Human Destiny.* (2018, July 10). Inner Traditions.

33. "History – McCoole's at the Historic Red Lion Inn." (2022, February 7). McCoole's at the Historic Red Lion Inn.

Retrieved March 26, 2022, from https://www.mccoolesredlion inn.com/history/

34. Adams, J. (1800, May). "Proclamation of Pardons to Those Engaged in Fries Rebellion." From *National Archives.* https://millercenter.org/the-presidency/presidential-speeches/may-21-1800-proclamation-pardons-those-engaged-fries-rebellion

35. "History | Seven Stars Inn." (n.d.). Retrieved September 15, 2022, from https://www.sevenstarsinn.com/history/

36. "Ghost Tours of Haunted Brinton Lodge." (n.d.). Retrieved September 15, 2022, from https://brintonlodge.com/ghosttours

37. "Downtown Bethlehem Hotel Ghosts." (2019, October 22). Historic Hotel Bethlehem. Retrieved August 12, 2021, from https://www.hotelbethlehem.com/ghosts/

38. "The Sun Inn Preservation Association – Museum/Walking Tour." (2022, July 28). The Sun Inn. Retrieved June 1, 2022, from https://suninnbethlehem.org/museum/

39. Dolan, F. X. (2007, August 8). *Eastern State Penitentiary (PA) (Images of America)* (Illustrated). Arcadia Publishing.

40. "History of Eastern State." (n.d.). Eastern State Penitentiary Historic Site. Retrieved September 10, 2022, from https://www.easternstate.org/research/history-eastern-state

41. Meler, C. (2022, June 3). "America's First Zoo | History in the Making." Philadelphia Zoo. Retrieved September 29, 2022, from https://philadelphiazoo.org/about-the-zoo/

42. "Pottsgrove Manor." Montgomery County, PA – Official Website. (n.d.). Retrieved September 29, 2022, from https://www.montcopa.org/930/Pottsgrove-Manor

43. "Fonthill Castle." (n.d.). Mercer Museum & Fonthill Castle. Retrieved December 2, 2021, from https://www.mercermuseum.org/about/fonthill-castle/

44. Mercer, H. C. (2015, October 6). *November Night Tales.* Valancourt Books.

45. Rettew, B. (2022, February 5). "Iconic Baldwin's Book Barn in West Chester celebrating its 200th anniversary." Daily Local. Retrieved September 15, 2022, from https://www.dailylo cal.com/2022/02/04/iconic-baldwins-book-barn-in-west-chester-celebrating-its-200th-anniversary/

46. Collins, Simon. (2001). "Frick's Lock Village: Historic Park Feasibility Study." Frens and Frens, LLC.

47. Abplanalb, PhD, Kathleen M. (2010, March). "Historical and Architectural Survey of Frick's Lock Historic District." Frens and Frens, LLC. Retrieved September 30, 2022, from https://eastcoventry-pa.gov/vertical/sites/%7BA2FA46C5-686F-4B16-8376-0BDF39FCC483%7D/uploads/Fricks_Lock _Report_101510(1).pdf

48. Cywinski, M. (2022, January 6). "Site of the Rhoads Opera House Fire." Atlas Obscura. Retrieved January 7, 2022, from https://www.atlasobscura.com/places/rhoads-opera-house-fire-building

49. Undefined. [69News WFMZ-TV]. (2020, January 13). *The Rhoads Opera House Fire: Legacy Of A Tragedy [Full Documentary]* [Video]. YouTube. Retrieved September 15, 2022, from https://www.youtube.com/watch?v=iSCGwWb9zfE

50. "What Happened at Valley Forge – Valley Forge National Historical Park" (n.d.). US National Park Service. Retrieved September 29, 2022, from https://www.nps.gov/vafo/learn/historyculture/valley-forge-history-and-significance.htm

51. "Haunted Lancaster: The Ghost of General 'Mad Anthony' Wayne and his Missing Bones." (2021, November 9). Uncharted Lancaster. Retrieved September 29, 2022, from https://unchartedlancaster.com/2021/10/10/haunted-lancaster-mad-anthonys-missing-ghostly-bones/

52. "Chapter Four: The Park Commission Triumphs." (n.d.). NPS: Valley Forge National Historic Park. Retrieved August 18, 2022, from https://www.nps.gov/parkhistory/online_books/vafo/treese/treese4a.htm

53. "Historic Chicago Hotel." (n.d.). Congress Plaza Hotel. Retrieved September 29, 2022, from https://www.congress plazahotel.com/history

54. "Death Leap of 3 Refugees Laid Persecution." (1939, August 5). *Chicago Tribune*, 10.

55. "Sealed Room 1252 on 12th Floor of Congress Plaza Hotel." (2022, August 28). The Haunted Places. Retrieved September 29, 2022, from https://thehauntedplaces.com/sealed-room-1252-on-congress-plaza-hotel-12th-floor

56. "The Restless Painting." (n.d.). Traveling Museum of the Paranormal & Occult. Retrieved June 28, 2022, from http://paramuseum.com/pieces/the-restless-painting/

57. Sacco, Robert G. (2019). "The Predictability of Synchronicity Experience: Results from a Survey of Jungian Analysts." *International Journal of Psychological Studies*. Canadian Center of Science and Education. 11 (3): 46–62.

58. "History Of Fort William Henry, Now A Kid-Friendly Attraction in Lake George NY." (2021, April 21). Fort William Henry Museum and Restoration. Retrieved October 4, 2022, from https://www.fwhmuseum.com/history/

59. Starbuck, D. R. (1991). "A Retrospective on Archaeology at Fort William Henry, 1952-1993: Retelling the Tale of The Last of the Mohicans." *Northeast Historical Archaeology*, 20(1), 8–25. https://doi.org/10.22191/neha/vol20/iss1/2

60. "Fort East Martello." (n.d.). Key West Art & Historical Society. Retrieved January 16, 2022, from https://www.kwahs.org/museums/fort-east-martello/visit

61. Harrison, B. (2021, October 27). *Undying Love: The*

Shocking True Key West Story of A Passion That Defied Death. HG&M Publishing.

62. Lewis, C. S. (2017, February 14). *The Four Loves* (Reissue). HarperOne.

ABOUT THE AUTHOR

Mallory Cywinski has her B.S. in Human Development and Family Studies from Penn State University, and she lives just outside Philadelphia, PA with her husband, son, daughter, and rescue dog. She is a paranormal investigator, content creator, and Halloween fanatic with a soft spot for YA Fantasy literature. Her writing has been featured in Volumes 1 & 2 of *The Feminine Macabre: A Women's Journal of All Things Strange and Unusual*, as well as on various online dark tourism blogs. She'd happily go miles out of her way for a peppermint oatmilk latte, preferably from a café with claims of a haunting. Follow her on Instagram, Facebook, TikTok, and YouTube @coffeebooksandghosts.

facebook.com/coffeebooksandghosts

instagram.com/coffeebooksandghosts

Made in United States
North Haven, CT
28 February 2023

33319451R00193